The Jim Dilemma

And I shall like it, whether anybody else does or not.
— Mark Twain, on **Adventures of Huckleberry Finn**

The Jim Dilemma

*Reading Race in **Huckleberry Finn***

Jocelyn Chadwick-Joshua

University Press of Mississippi
Jackson

Copyright © 1998 by University Press of Mississippi
Manufactured in the United States of America

01 00 99 98   4 3 2 1

The paper in this book meets the guidelines for permanence and
durability of the Committee on Production Guidelines for Book
Longevity of the Council on Library Resources.

Library of Congress Cataloging-in-Publication Data

Chadwick-Joshua, Jocelyn.
    The Jim dilemma : reading race in Huckleberry Finn / Jocelyn
Chadwick-Joshua.
        p. cm.
    Includes bibliographical references and index.
    ISBN 1-57806-060-5 (cloth : alk. paper). — ISBN 1-57806-061-3
(pbk. : alk. paper)
        1. Twain, Mark. 1835–1910.   Adventures of Huckleberry Finn.
2. Literature and society—United States—History—19th century.
3. Authors and readers—United States—History—19th century.
4. Twain, Mark, 1835–1910—Characters—Fugitive slaves.   5. Twain,
Mark, 1835–1910—Political and social views.   6. Twain, Mark.
1835–1910—Characters—Afro-Americans.   7. Satire, American—History
and criticism.   8. Fugitive slaves in literature.   9. Race relations
in literature.   10. Afro-Americans in literature.   I. Title.
PS1305.C45   1998
813'.4—dc21   98-25226
                                                              CIP

British Library Cataloging-in-Publication Data available

For my family—the Chadwicks, the Banks, and the Browns—whose legacy has always encouraged me to ask the hard questions and seek the truth

Contents

Acknowledgments

Robert S. Durpree, Dean Bishop, Shelley Fisher Fishkin, Jim Miller, David E. E. Sloane, David Bradley, Danielle Taylor-Guthrie, and John E. Grassie deserve more appreciation and admiration than I could ever give them for contributing to my writing this book. I must also express my sincere gratitude to each and every person at The Mark Twain Memorial in Hartford, CT. They encouraged me, asked pointed and pertinent questions, gave me access to vast research resources, including, most importantly, access to high school students and teachers around the country. I thank the hundreds of school districts, the thousands of students, and the hundreds of teachers whose ideas and questions helped to frame the premise of this book. I would also like to extend my appreciation to Mrs. Earsell Branch and Mrs. Shirley G. Huley of Vivian's Beauty Shop for their inexhaustible archive of *Jet* magazines and to R. Frank Lukner of the Dallas Institute of Humanities and Culture Bookstore for an unwavering willingness to help secure even the most difficult to find materials.

My unending thanks to my daughter, Cressyda, who was herself in high school while I was writing this book and who was my "living laboratory" when I had further questions. She is always a constant source of support and a rock-solid resource. My gratitude and never-ending love to my mother who stood as a sentinel outside of my study door, assuring uninterrupted segments of writing and research time.

My associate, F. Gregory Stewart, who has been closer to me than my right hand, deserves my sincere and heartfelt appreciation for his tenacity, his focus, and his incredible support during the final and seemingly endless editing sessions. Finally, I must acknowledge my editor and production editor at the University Press of Mississippi, Seetha A-Srinivasan and Anne Stascavage, without whose belief in me and this project, *The Jim Dilemma* would never have been realized.

Introduction

Blacks are the murderers, the rapists, the gang-bangers, where everything that is negative is [sic] society, why do I have to go to school and
be Jim too? Because whenever I read about the slave who is gullible
and stupid, that [stereotype] becomes a reflection of me, too.

Doron Flake, student, New Haven, Connecticut, public schools

We're tired of Nigger Jim sittin' in . . .

picket sign, Cathy Monterio, parent of a student in Tempe, Arizona

Much debate has surrounded Mark Twain's *Adventures of Huckleberry
Finn* since its publication in 1885, but none has been more pervasive,
explosive, and divisive than that surrounding the issue of race. Many
who do not view the book as racist often see only Jim's humanity and
"pal" relationship with Huck. Others, however, view the text as "the
most grotesque example of racist trash ever written" and see African
Americans as dehumanized, objectified, and stereotyped (Wallace, Editorial 146).[1] Yet a third group has emerged to assert that Twain's book
represents, as black poet and author Langston Hughes observes,
"a conscious (re)visioning of the South and the Southern slave."
To Hughes, Twain's books "punctured some of the pretenses of

the romantic Old South. The character of Jim in *Huckleberry Finn* . . . is considered one of the best portraits in American fiction of an unlettered slave clinging to the hope of freedom" (235). This volume was written to expand upon Hughes's contention.

Adventures of Huckleberry Finn has become in the twentieth century a required staple for American high school students—juniors, usually—who study a survey of American literature.[2] In its tenure it has been attacked in schools around the country—from San Jose, California, to New Haven, Connecticut—because of its perceived racist assertions. The NAACP in New York in 1957 sought to have the book banned in New York public schools because of "the excessive use of 'nigger'" (Wallace, "The Case Against *Huckleberry Finn*" 17). Miami-Dade Junior College removed *Adventures of Huckleberry Finn* from a course in 1969 for the same reason (Wallace, "The Case Against *Huckleberry Finn*" 17).[3] As teachers and supporters of this novel, we often ask how students can fail to comprehend and appreciate Jim. How can students and parents, even legislators, determine without reading the novel—without truly reading it—that it possesses racist overtones? How can readers of the novel miss Jim's and the other slaves' importance to the entire working out of the novel's plot tensions? Are readers deliberately closing their eyes to what Jim brings to the narrative? Why do Jim's strengths somehow also become grounds for his condemnation? Consider the constellation of his virtues: his sense of honor, ethics, loyalty, indomitable faith in the nuclear family (a faith that extends into guardianship of Huck Finn), masterful ability to manipulate language, sturdy sense of duty, grasp of the deep meaning of friendship, clear perception of himself as a man, unintimidating wisdom, desire to be self-reliant, and conscious awareness of taking risks. These traits are the marks of a hero.

For some readers, though, polarized by their racial preconceptions, Jim appears to be an Uncle Tom, an embarrassment, a minstrel. He seems so to the bright, sensitive (and angry) young man, Doron Flake, quoted above. He seems so to Doron's mother, educator Marcela Flake, who is among those who have sought to remove *Adventures of Huckleberry Finn* from school reading lists. And he seems that to Cathy Monterio, as the words quoted above from her picket sign make clear.[4] These parents are not alone in their desire to alleviate their children's discomfort at confronting the painful and debilitating effects of racism and slavery. But is censorship of *Adventures of Huckleberry Finn*, as they and others advocate, the most effective way to improve American racial perception?

As educators, we focus on maintaining the self-esteem of all students—both young and old, white and African American, northerner and southerner. And because we advocate continuing to include *Adventures of Huckleberry Finn* in the classroom, we must answer objections and concerns honestly and directly or else fail in our endeavor to keep this and similar works in high school and college classrooms. Jim is no murderer; Jim is no rapist; Jim is not a thief. He is no gangsta, nor is he gullible and stupid. Jim is nobody's fool. He endures, and he overcomes.

So, just what is Jim worth? Perhaps we should allow Twain's book to be removed from required reading lists, and even from libraries, without again looking at it closely, trying to ascertain just what Twain is expressing and, as importantly, how he expresses it. According to Ralph Ellison, African American literary critics at the time of the novel's publication did not even review it. Why make such an issue of this character? It would be all too easy simply to close our eyes, shut off our brains, and forget the cost society has paid in the past for the destruction of ideas. But we cannot. The issue of race is central to America's future, and such a denial or avoidance of America's past would necessarily result in what Toni Morrison describes as "a sure way to have a truncated life, a life that has no possibilities in it" ("I Come from a People Who Sing All the Time" 7). We Americans, and particularly African Americans, need to find a clearer understanding of who we were, as wonderful and as painful as our history is, so that we can more successfully determine what we wish to become. Those of us who actually have ties to the southern slave heritage, as do I, find that *Adventures of Huckleberry Finn* compels us to confront what I call the "Jim dilemma": the need to distinguish a richly positive and generous humanity from the confusing crosscurrents of prejudice that obscure it. The challenge to face these sensitive issues offers us all a great opportunity to realize our highest potential as a thoughtfully integrated culture.

The Jim Dilemma seeks earnestly to address the concerns and issues of opponents to the continued presence of *Adventures of Huckleberry Finn* in the classroom, both parents and literary critics. As nineteenth-century scholar Anna Julia Cooper has observed, great American literature is that written by writers who dipped their pens "in the life blood of their own nation and pictured out its own peculiar heart throbs and agonies [to the extent] that the [whole] world cared to listen" (178). The paradox hidden within this dictum, Cooper continues, is that "[n]o Shakespeare arose to distill [sic] from [the southern slaves'] unmatched personality and unparalleled situations the exalted poesy and crude grandeur of an immortal Caliban" (175). Slave narratives, crudely powerful though some of these are, did not fulfill this purpose, for they speak of success and escape amid hardship. Some African American fiction in the early nineteenth-century approaches Cooper's ideal, but in general the genre was limited, particularly by stereotyped portrayals of African Americans that persisted far into the twentieth century. Rarely did African American authors write three-dimensionally about the life of the runaway slave whose attempt to escape is unsuccessful.

With *Adventures of Huckleberry Finn*, then, the depiction of the southern and northern African American within the realistic context of nineteenth-century America, pre–Civil War and post-Reconstruction, first occurs. Ernest Hemingway in 1935 made the now-renowned statement that "all modern literature comes from one book by Mark Twain called *Huckleberry Finn*" (22). Although Hemingway does not focus on Jim, I propose that we can come to understand Twain's focus on Jim, and that we can find in the theme of the fugitive slave and the hypocrisy of change, a unique window of opportunity to explore the issue of race through fiction. Furthermore, I suggest that, unlike Hemingway, we can through the medium of the Jim dilemma even find important meanings in the ending of the novel.

Adventures of Huckleberry Finn panoramically chronicles the plight of the runaway male slave, the slave community, the slave family, and the vision and indefatigable hope of this American. Against him is a South that is both proslavery, the progenitor of Jim Crow, and hypocritical in its values. More complexly, however, this chronicle is one whose conclusion questions the *readers* and *their* notions of what freedom means. What does it cost? Through Twain's portrayal of Jim and the other slaves, the African American slave emerges without what Langston Hughes disparaged as the romanticization of the South and southern slavery.

*   *   *

The Jim Dilemma seeks to explore *Adventures of Huckleberry Finn* more closely not because it requires more work than other literary texts but merely because it requires at least as much, and not less. Some sophistication must be developed to appreciate Twain's rendering of the African American presence and voice. Twain made an important decision to render all the characters through their appropriate southern dialect. Naturally, this decision adds to the novel's verisimilitude. More importantly, not allowing Jim to express himself in his own way would have defeated the novel's purpose and would indeed have diminished Jim's character. By allowing us to see what we see, and to hear Jim's voice, Twain enhances the whole notion of the southern slave's integrity and self-reliance in the face of the grotesque predicament that the "milder" forms of slave plantation life created.

Misinterpretations of Jim—who he really is, and how he makes modern African Americans feel—have filled not only the platforms of public debate but also academic journals, critical anthologies, and conference seminars. On the basis of these misinterpretations, which arise from misreading or not reading the novel or from watching the vacuous film versions of it, opponents of the novel believe that Jim is never actually in control of his own voice or presence. Rather, he is seen to function merely as the humorous mimic of Huck Finn. Yet, he is far more, to a careful reader, than the fool to Tom Sawyer or the other white men and women he encounters. Jim and Huck's South believed in the myth of the ignorant darkey perpetuated by slaveholders and slavery sympathizers. They habitually cast slave men and women in the subordinate roles of children. Literature of the time portrayed this human tragedy in dialogue, description, and plot action—as, for example, did Harriet Beecher Stowe's *Uncle Tom's Cabin* and Joel Chandler

Harris's *Uncle Remus Tales*. Twain's work does not stop with this picture, however, but elaborates through burlesque the price that Jim, the man, must pay in trying to escape the snares of slavery.

The Jim Dilemma seeks to create an environment conducive to discussing the real racial sensitivity informing this novel. In this discussion, I hope to include those who are not as familiar with Twain's style or his depiction of African Americans; those who have not read Twain since high school or college; and those who have never read this novel at all but who, nevertheless, object to its being taught. I hope this book will be a useful tool and reference for those who are already steeped in this novel and the debates it has engendered. I also hope that a refocusing on Jim and other African Americans depicted in this novel will provide some readers with a new reason for (re)reading this important work.

Chapter One, "Reading Race: A Dilemma," outlines some of the major points of literary critics who have taken a position for or against *Adventures of Huckleberry Finn*. As a foundation for discussing Twain's specific accomplishments in the novel, it also examines the book in terms of several broader literary concepts: the relationship between writer and audience and the ways in which Twain reaches both nineteenth- and twentieth-century readers; the ways in which Twain fills a gap left by slave narratives and African American fiction; and the ways in which Jim fulfills the role of the traditional hero. Countering charges of racism, this chapter points to significant incidents in Twain's life that support the view that his goals for *Adventures of Huckleberry Finn* were not racist. Twain's work is also discussed as historical commentary.

Chapter Two, "You Can't Learn a Nigger to Argue: Verbal Battles," discusses Twain's use of the classical satiric device, the logomachy. Many misconceptions about Twain's work generally, and Jim in particular, result as a failure to recognize and acknowledge the conventions of satire at work in *Adventures of Huckleberry Finn*. These misconceptions are, in part, an outgrowth of popular depictions of Jim in the movies, a character far removed from Twain's creation. This chapter examines Twain's initial construction of the slave quarter and Jim as the representative metaphor for the runaway slave. This section also explores the concept of community, one's recognition within that community, and the subsequent relationships that exist between Huck and Jim; Jim and Tom; Miss Watson, Huck and Pap; and Pap and free African Americans, represented here through the free Professor from the North. Jim, the counteragent to Huck's earlier indoctrination at the hands of Miss Watson and the widow, provides the necessary contrast and alternative through his and Huck's verbal battles. Their carefully styled exchanges actually make possible Huck's journey into discovery and reevaluation.

Chapter Three, "In the Dark, Southern Fashion: Encounters with Society," focuses on the critical midsection of the novel, a section that some critics feel moves Jim out of the primary action of the novel, thereby diminishing his voice and presence. This chapter demonstrates that the middle of the novel actually amplifies Jim's voice and presence, allowing Huck to experience for the first time other southern slaves and their network of communication. Most analyses of this novel overlook the other African Americans. This chapter looks more closely at the important roles these characters play in relation to Jim and Huck, as well as to Twain's overall theme. We also see Huck encounter what he clearly recognizes as the quintessence of southern aristocracy. Huck's intimate contact with the Grangerfords and Shepherdsons moves him to begin the questioning process, focusing on the logic of inexplicable brutality and on the inhumanity of a blood feud within a social class that is supposed to behave differently. We see Huck reevaluating previously held "truths" that the widow, Miss Watson, and his community have taught him.

Chapter Four, "Whah Is de Glory? The (Un)Reconstructed South," examines Huck's adjustments to the new ideas emerging in his consciousness. For the first time the moral and ethical rightness and naturalness of slavery become a dilemma for Huck. The voices of religious and social authority up to this point have always controlled Huck. Now they also undergo substantial transformation. More importantly, this chapter reexamines what critics have identified as the failed last chapters; it places the final portion of the novel within the structural metaphor of Reconstruction and post-Reconstruction, periods that Twain felt were not successful in their vision. Tom's reappearance signals the still (un)reconstructed South, for he sees no problem in using Jim as a vehicle for having fun and adventure. While some critics contend that Huck's complicity in Tom's "evasion" diminishes his earlier resolve, I assert that Huck remains true and consistent to the goal of freeing Jim, thereby assuming the role of the (re)constructing South. Jim completes the realistic and rather dark picture of the progress and promise of Reconstruction. Jim universally represents the southern ex-slave whose future and anticipated quality of life are at best questionable—given the pervasive economic, social, and political conditions in the South during the late 1880s.

Without the final third of this novel, Twain's analysis and exploration of such abstract concepts as freedom, inhumanity, individuality, family, and loyalty would be irreparably lost. Chapter Four explores the realities of Huck's realizing that justice and fair play are not necessarily the results of heroic and commendable acts. When he witnesses Jim's return in "rotten, heavy" chains and sees him placed once more in confinement with only bread and water as his reward, he understands that all in life is not balanced. To Huck and to all around him, including Jim, Jim is a captured runaway slave. Only Tom Sawyer possesses the real truth regarding Jim's situation. What must not be overlooked or minimalized is Huck's resoluteness to honor his choice of helping Jim.

Tom's conscious deception and equally conscious disregard for Jim's visibility and humanity both reveal the dilemma of indifference, ethnic intolerance, and continual denial of basic human rights, basic rights afforded even the lowliest white. But more profound than the dark and foreboding canopy of apathy and inhumanity in the conclusion is Twain's final rendering of Jim. Functioning as parallel and substantive themes, with equal strength, Jim's heroism, his self-reliance, his tenacity, and his assertion of choice emerge clearly and indisputably. So, with this duality framing the final chapters, the question becomes whether Tom's deception and his uninhibited revelation symbolize the final, resonant theme in this novel, as many opponents assert. I think not.

Although Jim does go back in chains and does suffer terribly not only at the hands of the Phelpses but at the hands of Tom Sawyer himself, his sacrifice, his deliberate decision to be quiet when brought back, and his sentiments, as expressed in the last chapter, all combine to reinforce not Tom and the ruse but Jim and his humanity and resourcefulness. It is this rethinking of the southern slave that is the true visionary center of this novel. Once a student listening to a lecture asked me, "Is Huck still a racist at the end of the novel?" The more significant question raised by the conclusion is one that Twain posed to his nineteenth-century audience as well as to us: In the face of the cancerous cruelty of the peculiar institution, what will it take to move humanity from passive complacency to active, even risky, opposition in order to effect significant change?

In the winter of 1995 and early spring of 1996 a concerned adult in a Texas school district sought to ban Twain's works. Why? She said that his work has "no intellectual value. It's fiction, stuff we're trying to forget. . . . That time has gone. This is a new day" (qtd. in Appleton 31a). But is the day as new as she thinks? The Mississippi House of Representatives only officially voted to end slavery and ratify the Thirteenth Amendment in March 1995. How could this issue have remained unfinished business for 130 years? To deny one's heritage and legacy is to deny oneself, to invite invisibility and impending disaster for our young, for what is their anchor, or mooring? We must arm our children to survive in a world where racism does still exist. We must teach them about their American ancestral faces and voices, the faces and voices of Jim, Jack, the free northern Professor, the slave family, and the slave women and men whom Huck observes as the lynch mob moves toward Colonel Sherburn's home. Shelley Fisher Fishkin, in *Lighting Out for the Territory: Reflections on Mark Twain and American Culture*, states that Twain and *Adventures of Huckleberry Finn* provide a continuing forum for this discussion and recovery. I agree. In fact, this novel adds its voice to those of the nineteenth-century African American periodicals that stressed this same need for remembering: *The Colored American*, *The Anglo-African*, *The Elevator*, *Douglass' Monthly*, *Freedman's Journal*, and *The Mirror of Liberty*.

Jim is no Uncle Tom; he is no handkerchief-head nigger—and I use the slur deliberately because it is too often used today by African Americans to denigrate any African American who articulates a view different from the "perceived majority" of African Americanism. I stand instead with such figures as Ann Plato, Anna Julia Cooper, Zora Neale Hurston, George Schuyler, Malcolm X, after his pilgrimage to Mecca, and, more recently, with small and quiet but clear murmurings, Martin Luther King, Jr. Jim is a man, a father, a husband, a slave who decides to run toward an ideal—freedom—in a country where his mask and double voice are his survival tools. Because it is uncomfortable and even painful to revisit this period closely, American readers, particularly African American readers, often assume Jim's mask is nonrecognition. Their response is rejection.

Until we embrace Jim and all that he represents, however, we will forever pale as a people, will be historically colorless. We will lack the very life's blood vital to any culture's and individual's survival. And as such, we run the risk of blinding our children to their own history and legacy, thereby creating future generations bereft of the sight necessary for historical reflection and cultural lineage. In *Figures in Black: Words, Signs, and the "Racial" Self,* Henry Louis Gates speaks of the necessity of recognition. African Americans have to rediscover our voice and our face so as to reclaim our history. Our predecessors attempted to begin this reclamation—African American writers like Frederick Douglass, Phillis Wheatley, and Harriet E. Wilson. Other nineteenth-century writers such as Mark Twain, Frances Harper, William Wells Brown, Pauline Hopkins, Charlotte-Forten Grimké, Charles Chesnutt, John Greenleaf Whittier, and Ralph Waldo Emerson attempted to recreate for their audiences voices of people who had an inalienable right to be heard and experienced. On this universal note Ralph Ellison is quite clear:

Times change but these possessions must endure forever—not simply because they define us as a group, but because they represent a further instance of man's triumph over chaos. You know the skins of those thin-legged girls who faced the mob in Little Rock marked them as Negro but the spirit which directed their feet is the old universal urge toward freedom. For better or worse, whatever there is of value in Negro life is an American heritage and as such it must be preserved. . . . As for the writer's necessity of cashing in on the pain undergone by my people (and remember I write of the humor as well), writing is my way of confronting, often for the hundredth time, that same pain and that same pleasure. It is my way of seeing that it not be in vain. ("That Same Pain" 103)

The Jim Dilemma seeks to address what a very special friend said to me as I was in the throes of writing this book. I quote it here because it seems to me to telescope the purpose and hope for this work: What better way to channel [one's] energy than to help increase tolerance, understanding, and most important of all, acceptance of one another? It is my hope that this book will accomplish such worthy and necessary aspirations.

The Jim Dilemma

Reading Race

A Dilemma

In "An American Dilemma," Ralph Ellison asks whether "American
Negroes are simply the creation of White men or have they at least
helped to create themselves out of what they have found around them"
(301). Mark Twain compels the reader of *Adventures of Huckleberry
Finn* to address not only this question but the question of visibility and
legacy. The novel challenges the white reader to learn about and experience a traumatic and debasing period in American history, as well as
discovering the unique circumstances of American literary history. At
the same time, Twain presents to this audience a covenant of hope in
the unlikeliest of places with the unlikeliest of characters. For Twain's
African American audience, the novel necessitates if not a complete
celebration for and recovery of the slave of the South at least an acknowledgment of the traits that defined and molded a people, a spirit,
and a vision of their next-century's progeny: resilience, tenacity, resourcefulness, and passion—passion for freedom, family, and ultimately, a passion for the American ideal.

Adventures of Huckleberry Finn explores the sensitive issues with
which the African American middle class of the twentieth century has
privately struggled. When any fiction attempts to examine these
themes, particularly when written by a person who is not African
American, the response has been swift and predictable. Rightly or

wrongly, we initially judge the narrative suspect. Opponents usually assume the characters to be stereotypes or caricatures. It is also usually assumed that the readers, particularly children, will be insulted or harmed by the exposure to such fiction. To be sure, African Americans have had a right to be wary during the nineteenth and twentieth centuries about literature that contained racist underpinnings. Unfortunately, meritorious works have been caught up in the wide accusation of racism, *Adventures of Huckleberry Finn* being a prime example. Mark Twain has not been the only writer to be vilified by opponents; works written by women of color with similarly challenging themes endure similar suspicion and attempts at censorship. Twain, like all great writers, refuses to allow the luxury of nonthinking, of noninvolvement. He refuses to allow us to be bereft of necessary truths, painful though they are. He is neither too polite nor too fearful to weave a narrative that, as Toni Morrison observes, "obliges us to embrace a disrupting darkness before its eyes" (*Playing in the Dark* 91).

Black middle-class parents and racial activists, we must note, are not the only opposition seeking to manipulate what is read. Another equally important group involved in textual subversion are the writers of specialized critical discourse.[1] A number of literary critics oppose the novel, saying that it fails in a number of ways, many of them not at all racial. Van Wyck Brooks in *The Ordeal of Mark Twain* (1920) cites Twain's exposure to the East as a reason for his not realizing his fullest potential in this novel, by making it too mild in tone. Leo Marx's "Mr. Eliot, Mr. Trilling, and Huckleberry Finn" (1953) asserts that the last twelve chapters fail—and weaken the overall effectiveness of the novel. In the last twenty-five years, attention has focused more directly on the novel's racial posture, and thus on Jim. Neil Schmitz's "Twain,

Huckleberry Finn, and the Reconstruction" (1971) claims that Jim at the novel's conclusion is impotent and "the object of devious schemes" (18). Forrest G. Robinson's "The Characterization of Jim in *Huckleberry Finn*" (1988) contends that although Jim does reach the status of manhood in the novel, he eventually reverts to a two-dimensional character, gullible and superstitious. James Cox's "A Hard Book to Take" (1985) never actually asserts a strong position on the character of Jim, placing him, consequently, in ambiguity. One of the most outspoken critics, John Wallace, in *"Huckleberry Finn*: Literature or Racist Trash?"* (1991) and "The Case Against *Huckleberry Finn*" (1992), unwaveringly asserts that Jim functions as a minstrel and that the teaching of this novel, with its use of "nigger," does nothing more than to perpetuate the teaching of racism in America's classroom.

Some literary critics express concerns that *Adventures of Huckleberry Finn* fails to depict Jim consistently. These concerns have been addressed most clearly to the nonacademic public in Jane Smiley's 1996 *Harper's* article, "Say It Ain't So, Huck: Second Thoughts on Twain's *Adventures of Huckleberry Finn*." Smiley's scattershot objections range from assertions of Twain's inherent racism to his inability to portray the African American realistically, to his conscious desire to berate the African American with his use of "nigger," to his stylistic duplicity in elevating Jim to a level of equality only to dash him once more to a status of inferiority and slavery in what many of the novel's detractors identify as the weakest and most racist section in the novel—the last twelve chapters.

Those of us who represent the case in favor of *Adventures of Huckleberry Finn* remain unshaken in our position. As Wayne C. Booth in *The Company We Keep: An Ethics of Fiction* articulates, the true literary scholar in defense of this book makes every effort to maintain an ethical balance. Booth himself, who admires the novel, revisits it from a different perspective when a colleague, Paul Moses, reveals his strong reservations about teaching it. To these reservations, Booth appropriately responds that such opposition provides an effective and productive environment for scholarly debate. As Morrison echoes in *Playing in the Dark*, Booth holds that such debate facilitates ethical academic responses and reminds us that "no simple, definitive conclusions lie ahead" (3-7). But it is actually William Dean Howells, Mark Twain's friend, who perceives the book's deepest sensibility. Howells's review of the novel expresses the heart of Twain scholarship as it relates specifically to *Adventures of Huckleberry Finn*: "[T]he Southwest lives in that book, as it lives nowhere else, with its narrow and rude conditions, its half savage heroism, its vague and dim aspiration, its feuds and its fights, its violence, its squalor, its self-devotion, all in shadow of that horrible cloud of slavery darkening both the souls and the minds of men. There are moments of almost incredible pathos in the book . . . and also of a lofty joy, which is not the less sublime because of the grotesque forms it takes" (qtd. in Twain, *Mark Twain-Howells Letters* 117). Howells's comment establishes the "two Souths" in which Jim lives throughout the novel, as evidenced by Huck and the people he meets along the Mississippi—the brutality juxtaposed with humanity.

Noted modern critics and scholars concur with Howells. Lionel Trilling's introduction to the Rinehart edition (1948) cites the novel as "one of the central documents of American culture" (311). Ralph Ellison's "Change the Joke and Slip the Yoke" (1958) is among the first essays to discuss the minstrel mask behind which Jim operates and through which Jim's dignity and humanity emerge (39-40). Nat Hentoff's *The Day They Came to Arrest the Book* (1985) asserts that

Twain's book is a strategical masterpiece in that Twain allows an adolescent not only to relate an important story but also to find a father figure in the slave Jim. In a recent conversation, Hentoff stated that this novel is not only the least racist he has ever read but that the character of Jim is one that signals a redeeming hope for the future health of society. Justin Kaplan's introduction to the Random House comprehensive edition of *Adventures of Huck Finn* (1992) asserts that one could not imagine American literature without engaging in this book and its journey into the dark passages of slavery and racism. And make no mistake, *Adventures of Huckleberry Finn* insists that we travel with Jim and Huck down the river of racism and inhumanity. Like Ellison, scholar David Smith in "Huck, Jim, and American Racial Discourse" (1992) focuses on Twain's Jim and provides one of the most comprehensive studies of this character. Shelley Fisher Fishkin's *Was Huck Black?* (1993) explores the stylistic impact that African American voices had on *Huckleberry Finn*. Fishkin argues that the African American voices Twain heard as he matured manifest themselves in Huck Finn—his use of the language, his moral code, and his actions. The list does indeed go on. Yet recently at the 1997 Mark Twain Symposium in Hartford, Connecticut, we can find evidence that the debate surrounding this novel has only increased. Although this symposium, "Mark Twain: Allegory in Writing," was intended to focus on twenty-nine volumes in Oxford University Press's new editions of Twain's works, discussion returned essentially to this singular, pivotal book.

The Twain symposium's focus seems predictable because the very purpose of literature—great literature like this novel—is to inspire, to agitate, and, it is hoped, to insist on change when necessary and to remind when we so desperately seek to forget.[2] Great literature specifically causes readers to explore, reexamine, reevaluate, and, perhaps, reconstruct firmly held views and ideas. *Adventures of Huckleberry Finn*, with its themes and its characters like Jim and Huck, creates this kind of intellectual tempest. Jim, representing America's greatest unfinished social issue, must arrive at, if not become, the center of the tempest's energy.

The time has long since been propitious to reexamine the text of this work in light of difference. The difference cited here is a rhetorical one that acknowledges the dissimilarity that time and space have created between the book's nineteenth- versus twentieth-century readers, Euro-Americans versus African Americans and other people of color, northerners versus southerners, and those of free African American ancestry versus those of slave lineage. The writer's purpose is to convey effectively the narrative's literal and symbolic messages. If Twain has been successful, every reader will reach some degree of understanding of the writer's literal message as that message unfolds through the characters, though complete and unqualified agreement by the reader with the text's emotional message may not be accomplished.[3] This understanding is often referred to as identification, meaning that, despite what happens in the text, the reader will recognize some facets of the action, reactions, and developments that pertain to his or her own time and experience, either directly or indirectly. With *Adventures of Huckleberry Finn*, for example, while many readers will have had no direct experience with child abuse or slavery or a lynch mob, Twain captures the essence of each of these realities so that readers can acknowledge, or identify with, each incident even though they may wish to reject them or deny them for personal reasons.

Adventures of Huckleberry Finn today confronts a number of African American readers who, for the most part, cannot embrace and acknowledge one of the central characters without extreme anxiety. Twentieth-century opponents may not give Jim his due recognition and presence because even Jim describes himself in the grotesquely distorted ideology of his time and place. Jim—Miss Watson's slave and a runaway throughout most of the novel—realizes that he is not worthless as he has been led to believe but rather is quite valuable, valuable to the tune of eight hundred dollars. Being rich to Jim supplants the typical definition a student would like attributed to human well-being. Owning himself and being worth a substantial sum begins his personal removal from marginality and invisibility. Jim declares, "Yes—en I's rich now, come to look at it. I owns myself, en I's wuth eight hund'd dollars. I wisht I had de money, I wouldn' want no mo'" (73). The lack of significant reaction by students to his statement—unless teachers have properly prepared them for the narrative's themes—proves that just as students need a context in which to understand European writers and other American writers, they also need guidance with this work in both high school and college. Satire distorts values, and Jim is affected as much as is Huck's conscience.

Buying and selling an individual is a remote idea to modern students.[4] Recognition and validation of the historical plight Jim represents are, in reality, impossible to individuals of *any* ethnicity whose greatest exposure to not being free is having a curfew, curtailment of telephone privileges, or even experiencing late–twentieth-century racial, cultural, or gender bias. This is not to dismiss the inestimable significance or sacrifice of people such as Medgar Evers, Martin Luther King, Jr, Malcolm X, or Rosa Parks, harassed because of their race, but most adolescents and young adults today have no first-hand experience of freedom denied as the southern slave did. Students' reaction to Jim's statement of owning himself, and his "worth," then, is a nonreaction until the teacher aids them in understanding how the slave trade practiced in the South affected the African American slave's self-perception.

Although many sources exist, primary and secondary, that detail the slave trade in America and the southern slaves' view of themselves, I will focus here on only two: first, Jim's own statement to Huck when they miss Cairo and, second, the 1829 decisive commentary of North Carolina Supreme Court Judge Thomas Ruffin. When both Huck and Jim are certain that they have missed Cairo, Huck simply states, "Jim was awful disappointed, but I said never mind, Cairo would be the next place, I reckoned . . . . I begun to suspicion something. So did Jim" (129). Like today's adolescents and young adults, Huck's distance and lack of familiarity with Jim's experiences, hopes, and feelings preclude significant understanding of his past and the enormity of this event in relation to it. Jim responds not to Huck specifically but rather to a larger audience: "Doan' less' talk about it, Huck. Po' niggers can't have no luck. I awlus 'spected dat rattle-snake skin warn't done wid its work" (129).

As a corollary, Justice Ruffin's statement reveals not simply one more justification for slavery but, more importantly, why slaves had to develop protective layers to shield their real slave selves and why so many prepared themselves for defeat—just in case: "The end [of slavery] is the profit of the master, his security, and public safety; the subject [the slave], one doomed in his own person, and his posterity, to live without knowledge, and without the capacity to make anything his own, and to toil that another may reap the fruits. . . such services can only be expected from one who has no will of his own; who surrenders his will in implicit obedience is the consequence only of uncontrolled authority over the body. . . . The power of the master must be absolute to render the submission of the slave perfect" (quoted in Schwarz 71).

Benjamin Schwarz used this excerpt in an *Atlantic Monthly* article to explain Thomas Jefferson's position with regard to the Constitution and slavery. Incidentally, Ruffin supplies us with reason for the myth of inherent slave docility. In contrast, Jim's proclamation to Huck is not one of servile docility and blind acceptance. Jim's comment, rather, affirms that whenever slaves assert themselves and attempt controlling their own destiny, they must necessarily be prepared for complete defeats or substantial impediments.

Far from being an Uncle Tom statement, then, Jim's redefinition of wealth functions as the novel's central focus, since he realizes that he is indeed worth something. Money, after all, is a great leveler in that all cultures recognize and affirm this fact. Critics of this novel, however, read into this statement Twain's alleged racist intentions and Jim's equally alleged weakness.

Nowhere is this sentiment regarding the significance of owning one's self and the realization of it rendered more poignantly than in Toni Morrison's Pulitzer Prize–winning novel, *Beloved*. Relying, like Twain, on supporting characters to elucidate and amplify themes, Morrison uses Sethe's husband, Halle, and mother-in-law, Baby Suggs. Halle, a slave himself with an ever-increasing family, buys his mother's freedom. What makes the following scene so riveting and significant lies with not only Baby Suggs's discovery and subsequent definition of slavery but her age. Like mature Jim, Baby Suggs is a mature woman whose children, born into that peculiar institution, are to her but tiny feet and hands—disconnected memories, painful memories. Because of what she has seen and experienced, Baby Suggs's definition of freedom carries with it agonies and profound insight un-matched by the young, even Halle. When Baby Suggs initially de-scends from the wagon that has delivered her to freedom, she thinks to herself: "What does a sixty-odd-year-old slavewoman who walks like a three-legged dog need freedom for? And when she stepped foot on free ground she could not believe that Halle [her son] knew what she didn't; that Halle, who had never drawn one free breath, knew that there was nothing like it in this world. . . . Something's the matter. What's the matter? What's the matter? she asked herself. She didn't know what she looked like and was not curious. But suddenly she saw her hands and thought with a clarity as simple as it was dazzling, 'These hands belong to me. These *my* hands.' Next she felt a knocking in her chest and discovered something else new: her own heartbeat. Had it been there all along? This pounding thing?" (141).

Not owning one's own hand or arm or heartbeat, for all students reading Twain's novel and for Huck Finn, himself, is unimaginable. Readers must explore and meditate on profound realizations of the consciousness that belongs to Jim and his fellow slaves, who are seen as purposefully evasive at the margins of the story's action. One must read and comprehend the literal meaning that Jim, as well as Baby Suggs, is communicating.[5]

Many teachers and others with whom I have spoken around the country proclaim exasperation that opponents to this novel simply "don't get it." They assert that Jim is, after all, the hero; what's the problem? One part of the problem is our inability to understand wholly the nature and persona of a hero of Jim's stature—an African American runaway slave, illiterate and, according to some, invisible. But if we examine for a moment classical critic Bernard Knox's clarifi-cation of a hero in conjunction with that of writer and critic Albert

Murray's, I think that we can comprehend more completely the unquestionably heroic stature Jim achieves throughout the narrative's forty-three chapters. In *The Heroic Temper: Studies in Sophoclean Tragedy*, Knox, writing on the plays of Sophocles, anticipates Jim's heroism in Grecian terms: "The Sophoclean characters are responsible, through their action and intransigence, for the tragic consequences. . . . Sophocles creates a tragic universe in which man's heroic action, free and responsible, brings him sometimes through suffering to victory but more often to a fall which is both defeat and victory at once; the suffering and the glory are fused in an indissoluble unity. Sophocles pits against the limitations on human stature great individuals who refuse to accept those limitations, and in their failure achieve a strange success. Their action is fully autonomous; for these actions and the results, the gods, who are the guardians of the limits the hero defies, bear no responsibility" (6). According to Albert Murray, "Heroism, which like the sword is nothing if not steadfast, is measured in terms of the stress and strain of the obstacles it overcomes. Thus difficulties and vicissitudes which beset the potential hero on all sides not only threaten his existence and jeopardize his prospects; they also, by bringing out the best in him, serve his purpose. They make it possible for him to make something of himself. Such is the nature of every confrontation in the context of heroic action" (38).

Although Knox is examining classical tragedy and the polytheism of the Ancients and Murray the blues and the hero, both provide critical insight not only into Jim but into the psyche of the nineteenth-century slave and into the portrait woven in *Adventures of Huckleberry Finn*.[6] The opposite and disparate poles Knox cites are issues that were discussed in periodicals, fiction, and open forums during the nineteenth century: hope versus despair, especially the abject despair of the slave.

Murray's hero's sheer will, focus, and ability to use difficulty and impediments all relate to Jim and his journey throughout this novel. Both
the tragic hero and the blues hero, for that matter, all great and transformative heroes despite the age, share certain traits. Jim is the Sophoclean hero; he is also the blues hero. Once he makes up his mind, he
accepts no limitations—not the passing of Cairo; not his experiences
with other, less sympathetic white characters; not the obstacles confronting his purchasing his wife and two children.

Such resilience would necessarily include Jim's acknowledgment of
Jim Crow, the concept evolved in the South and subsequently spread
to the North. Twain was fully aware of the growth of Jim Crow sepa-
ratism from as early as 1869 through the period the novel was written,
and Jim's status as tragic hero is developed with this in mind. Further
rounding out Jim's role as hero, the creation of Jim Crow allows readers to witness Jim coping with a different, more tenacious and subtle
form of racism. With roots dating back to 1832, Jim Crow, according
to Lerone Bennett, Jr., shifted from being a song-and-dance caricature
of African Americans to becoming "a wall, a system, a way of separating people from people. Demagogue by demagogue, mania by mania,
brick by brick, the wall was built; and by the 1890s America was two
nations—one white, one black, separate and unequal. . . . One law led
to a hundred. One fear became a nightmare of ropes and chains and
signs" (256). Although we would like to believe that all will be well
after Tom reveals at the end of the novel his hidden truth that Jim has
been set free, the historical facts with which Twain would have been
most familiar do not bear out this idyllic hope. Twain, moreover, prepares the reader with a cascading style that foreshadows the novel's
final commentary on Jim Crow. Jim ultimately experiences freedom
through manumission only to have to experience the beginnings of

Jim Crow. Tom's "evasion" itself—the last twelve chapters of the book—places Jim in the paradoxical situation of failure and success, as Knox defines it, and the "difficulties and vicissitudes" to which Murray refers (6).

Finally, the gods, to whom Knox refers as the caretakers and architects of the hero's limits, emerge in the characters of Miss Watson, Tom Sawyer, Judge Thatcher, the king and duke, the Grangerfords and Shepherdsons, Aunt Sally, as well as the Wilks girls themselves, all symbols of the ultimate paradox of benevolent slavery. Jim's act of running away testifies to his rebellion against these caretakers, just as their response to him not as human being but as escaped chattle reveals their attitude toward slavery.

Huck, too, must initially recognize and acknowledge within himself what these authoritative powers mean to him. Only then can he effectively contrast them with and evaluate them against his growing exposure to Jim. For example, he tells Jim that the widow and Miss Watson do not lie, or he determines that because of their surroundings the Grangerfords are quality people. To realize the opposite as true decenters him psychologically and frightens him as well. But, as Knox asserts, when these "guardians" understand that Jim and Huck are functioning outside their prescribed parameters, they absolve themselves of responsibility for their actions, even recalcitrant Pap Finn. When Pap discovers that Huck really can read and write, he demands that Huck remain degraded and relinquish any notion he has about not continuing his "familial legacy": "And looky here—you drop that school, you hear? I'll learn people to bring up a boy to put on airs over his own father and let on to be better'n what *he* is. You lemme catch you fooling around that school again, you hear? Your mother couldn't read, and she couldn't write, nuther, before she died. None of the family couldn't, before *they* died. *I* can't; and here you're a-swelling yourself up like this. I ain't the man to stand it—you hear?" (40).

With the techniques of fiction at his command, Twain provides a novel that exceeds the range and focus of the slave narrative. If we look to Twain at the novel's inception and gestation, we do find that his prototype for the runaway slave merges slave narratives, biographical anecdotes about free people, and responses to the myth of the "happy darkey." We know historically that the slave narrative as a literary form was popular, initially in Europe and then in America, well before Stowe's *Uncle Tom*. Narratives, including *The Interesting Narrative of the Life of Olaudah Equiano, or Gustavas Vassa, The African* (1814), *The Narrative of the Life of Frederick Douglass* (1845), the transcribed narratives of Sojourner Truth (1850), Mary Prince (1831), and Henry "Box" Brown (1849), all contributed to the public's awareness of runaway slaves, their voices, and their trek to freedom. In many instances these and other slave escapes were recorded in the periodicals of the day—*The New York Times, Douglass' Monthly, The Liberator, The Mirror of Liberty*, and many others. While these periodicals printed accounts of these attempts, Frederick Douglass in *Douglass' Monthly* recounts a variety of them: "A Story of the Underground Railroad" (February 1857); "A Mother in Prison for Attempting to Free Her Children" (April 1859); "American Civilization Illustrated: A Great Slave Auction" (April 1859); "The Peculiar Institution—A Man Sells His Own Daughter" (February 1859). In every instance the runaways, successful and unsuccessful, share common traits: resolute concern about family; a drive to achieve almost superhuman acts because of their treatment; a desire for escape so deeply rooted that the methods for doing so grow more imaginative and dangerous; an unswerving faith, faith in the Almighty and faith in this country's promises, faith in the Union. Although southerners, to prevent the slave's very thought of running north or to Canada, created the myth of the abusive northerner, former southern slaves and free African Americans who traveled south would dispel this notion. Frances Harper's *Iola Leroy, or Shadows Uplifted* deals with this problem in the beginning chapters of her novel. Twain addresses this same issue through the appearance of the free professor in Chapter 6.

That Twain would be familiar with the popularity of the slave narrative and that he would have read some of the narratives is clear as is the fact that he knew some runaway slaves. He and Frederick Douglass, for example, were friends. On 12 January 1881, Samuel L. Clemens wrote a letter to President-elect Garfield, urging him to reappoint Douglass as Marshall of the District of Columbia: "A simple citizen may express a desire with all propriety, in the matter of a recommendation to office, and so I beg permission to hope that you will retain Mr. Douglass in his present office of Marshall of the District of Columbia, if such a course will not clash with your own preferences or with the expediences and interests of your administration. I offer this petition with peculiar pleasure and strong desire, because I so honor this man's high and blemishless character and so admire his brave, long crusade for the liberties and elevation of his race" (Twain, Letter). Knowing Frederick Douglass, as well as other free African Americans like Maryanne Cord (the model for Aunt Rachel in "A True Story") from many facets of life, profoundly affected Twain and provided ample resources for *Adventures of Huckleberry Finn*. In *Lighting Out for the Territory: Reflections on Mark Twain and American Culture*,

Shelley Fisher Fishkin examines these and other relationships Twain had with free African Americans and slaves, convincingly showing Twain's awareness of their situation in late nineteenth-century America.

The slave narrative in Britain and America did more than simply inform readers, including Twain, of the horrors and abuses of slavery. These narratives also shattered the stereotypes of the happy darkey, the happy mammy, the unfeeling and inferior nigger. The slave narratives motivated readers to revise their perceptions of the southern slave and of the African American in general. Twain likewise created Jim as one character to act in the novel as Huck's guide for enlightenment and inspiration. He then surrounded this character with a supporting cast of slaves and surface men. The character of Jim emerged from three distinctive men whom Twain met and with whom he developed profound friendships. They were Uncle Daniel, a slave owned by Twain's uncle when Twain was a boy spending his summers in Florida; John Lewis, a free-born African American who saved Twain's brother-in-law's family from certain injury and perhaps death in a runaway carriage; and George Griffin, Twain's butler while he was in residence at the Hartford home as well as on subsequent trips abroad.[7]

Each of the three African American men figuring in Jim's persona accomplished something with his life and forever affected the life of Samuel Clemens and, therefore, Mark Twain. George Griffin later became a member of the Union League Club for waiters and privately loaned money to those in need; John Lewis became a tenant worker at Quarry Farm and retired there, with a supplement from Twain himself; Uncle Daniel, owned by John Quarles of Quarry Farm, was freed in November 1855 at the age of fifty. Twain discussed his exposure to

Uncle Daniel and to his uncle's farm as one that he had not intended to allude to in a novel. He later explained how he did use it as the prototype for Aunt Sally's farm in Arkansas and for Uncle Daniel and the other slaves on this farm:

All the negroes were friends of ours, and with those of our age we were in effect comrades. I say in effect, using the phrase as a modification. We were comrades; color and condition imposed a subtle line which both parties were conscious of and rendered complete fusion impossible. We had a faithful and affectionate good friend, ally, and advisor in "Uncle Dan'l," a middle-aged slave whose head was the best one in the negro quarter, whose sympathies were wide and warm and whose heart was honest and simple and knew no guile. . . . spiritually, I have had his welcome company a good part of that time and have staged him in books under his own name and as "Jim," and carted him all around—to Hannibal, down the Mississippi on a raft and even across the Desert of Sahara in a balloon—and he has endured it all with the patience and friendliness and loyalty which were his birthright. It was on the farm that I got my strong liking for his race and my appreciation of certain of his fine qualities. This feeling and this estimate have stood the test of sixty years and more and have suffered no impairment. The black face is as welcomed to me now as it was then. *(The Autobiography of Mark Twain 5-6)*

After Uncle Daniel, John Lewis provided the most lasting and dramatic influence. Describing to William Dean Howells in a series of letters his initial impression of John Lewis, Twain shared a suspenseful and life-changing experience involving Lewis. One letter dramatically recounts the incident on 23 August 1877 with a runaway carriage, an event that Twain thought to be certain death for family members. Of the near-tragic incident and what he thought about Lewis as a man, Twain wrote,

Age about 45—& the most picturesque of men, when he sits in his fluttering work-day rags, humped forward into a bunch, with his aged slouch hat mashed down over his ears & neck. It is a spectacle to make the broken-hearted smile.

Lewis has worked mighty hard & remained mighty poor. At the end of each whole year's toil he can't show a gain of fifty dollars. He has borrowed money of the Cranes till he owed them $700—& he being conscientious & honest, imagine what it was to him to carry this stubborn, hopeless load [a load of manure] year in & year out. . . .

Lewis was still downtown, three miles away with his two-horse wagon, to get a load of manure. Lewis is the farmer (colored). He is of mighty frame and muscle, stocky, stooping, ungainly, has a good manly face and a clear eye. (*Mark Twain–Howells Letters*, vol. 1, 195)

What an image. I often ask students, individuals who articulate their hopes and dreams as wanting money, a large house, and a fast car or two, to explore what Twain is saying here about the relationship between happiness, work, and respect. For some African Americans, John Lewis and his "load of manure" represent the core of what we wish to deny, if not escape entirely. Lewis, his rickety wagon, and his team of horses, however, declare unequivocal pride in the act of working, tenacity, and accomplishment. Most importantly, John Lewis commands and demands respect as a folk hero of substantial dimensions.

Not for one second would Lewis be misconstrued as a poor, inarticulate, inferior "nigger" by anyone who is of a fair and open mind. Twain establishes Lewis's work ethic, his deliberateness, and his indomitable fortitude through simple description. He then shifts to the action. Ida, Charles Langdon's wife, their child, Julia, and the nurse Nora are in a runaway carriage with Twain in foot pursuit. "I ran on & on, still spared [this spectacle,] but saying to myself I shall see it at the turn of the road; they never can pass that turn alive" (196). With the tone of impending doom and despair, Twain recounted for Howells, "As I felt down the road, my impulse was to shut my eyes as I turned them to the right or left, and so delay for a moment the ghastly spectacle of mutilation and death I was expecting" (196). Instead, turning the corner, he finds the family safe thanks to John Lewis: "A miracle had been performed—nothing less. You see, Lewis—the prodigious, humped upon his front seat, had been toiling up, on his load of manure; he saw the frantic horse plunging down the hill toward him, on a full gallop, throwing his heels as high as a man's head at every jump. So Lewis turned his team diagonally across the road just at the 'turn,' thus making a V with the fence—the running horse could not escape that but must enter it. Then Lewis sprang to the ground & stood in this V. He gathered his vast strength, and with a perfect Creedmoor aim he seized the gray horse's bit as he plunged by and fetched him up standing!" (199).

This story is important because this relative stranger saved members of Twain's immediate family. Another importance lies in the effect this incident had upon Twain and his family. Lewis's unselfish heroism emerges in *Adventures of Huckleberry Finn*, first in the construction of Jim's character and later in Jim's heroic sacrifice to save Tom Sawyer. Twain told Howells, "I thought I ought to make a sort of record of it for future reference" (194). The Langdon family bestowed their appreciation on John Lewis, to which he responded, "But I beg to say, humbly, that inasmuch as divine providence saw fit to use me as a instrument for the saving of those presshious lives, the honner conferd upon me was greater than the feat performed" (199). Twain wrote that this portion of the letter from Lewis "contains a sentence which raises it to the dignity of literature" (199).

John Lewis's act, his humble response to the accolades heaped upon him, and his sentiments here typify the attitude of many African Americans in this country during the nineteenth century—unfettered, uncoerced, uncompromised recognition and selfless action. Make no mistake, Lewis does what he does not because he is an Uncle Tom, a handkerchief-head nigger, or uppity. He, Mr. John Lewis, elects— freely and consciously—to place his own life in jeopardy to save another's. What is the difference? Why is this incident so special? What Lewis does and Twain's presence as witness to it become part of a novel that over one hundred years after its publication will reach out, capture, and agitate the imaginations of generations who would otherwise know too little of the common man, the simple man, the honorable man Mr. John Lewis represents, a unique literary resource.

George Griffin, the third figure crucial for understanding Twain and his rendering of Jim, originally came to the Twain house to wash windows. As Twain wrote Howells, he "remained for half a generation" (*Mark Twain Notebooks and Journals*, vol. 2, 201). From Griffin, Twain's imagination gleaned other facets of Jim's character—honesty, loyalty, friendship, forthrightness, objective thinking, and wit. Living at home with the family, his room located next to Twain's study, George Griffin had a profound effect on Twain. Many times I have been told "authoritatively" that Mark Twain was a dyed-in-the-wool racist, a product of a racist South. These opponents find themselves unable to explain why a "racist" would allow Griffin so close as well as why Griffin would want to remain. To counter charges of racism levied against Twain, I have presented and will yet present alternative perspectives.

One undeniable piece of evidence is the sustained relationship

Twain forged with George Griffin.[8] Twain's third-floor study, flooded with sun and complete with veranda and billiard table as well as the more typical accoutrements of a writer, is flanked by a guest bedroom, and then a room that would become George Griffin's bedroom, also with a veranda. Why is the location important? Before Griffin assumed possession of the room, it was clearly designated as a guest room. He lived, actually lived, within the nucleus of the house rather than in some removed region or servants' quarters. His private space was three and one-half steps away from Twain's study. Would a racist writer place the object of his ire next to the very place of his creativity? Of equal interest, we must ask why Griffin would hang pictures of Twain's family in his room if in fact he was the target of such racism. Not even the most mistreated slave was required to hang pictures of the master in his quarters. It is an important indicator of their relationship that Griffin felt close enough to the family to bring them into his personal and private space in such a way.

Clearly, this relationship transcends the hierarchical one of employer-employee. It was not only a long and congenial, lasting from the late 1870s to the early 1890s; it also represented for Twain a framework within which to continue a psychological and sociological transformation begun much earlier. In an often-quoted statement that would generally be held as accurate for many southerners during the nineteenth century, Twain in his *Autobiography* states, "In my schoolboy days I had no aversion to slavery. I was not aware there was anything wrong about it. No one arraigned it in my hearing; the local papers said nothing against it; the local pulpit taught us that God approved it, that it was a holy thing and that the doubter need only look in the Bible if he wished to settle his mind—and then the texts were read aloud to make us make the matter sure; if the slaves themselves had an aversion to slavery they were wise and said nothing. In Hannibal we seldom saw a slave misused; on the farm never" (6).

This last statement is of particular significance in that it reflects Huck's own initial ambivalence to "benevolent slavery." Twain's adult awareness makes Jim and his story even more important in that this novel literally unravels the myth of the happy darkey under the aegis of the nonbrutal slave master or mistress. Slavery is, after all, slavery. Through the introduction of Jim and his owner, Miss Watson, Twain allows us to witness that from Jim's perspective and from Huck's she is not a brutal owner, but Twain also allows us to see that she is not beyond separating a family and selling Jim when the price is right: "Ole Missus—dat's Miss Watson—she pecks on me all de time, en treats me pooty rough, but she awlus said she wouldn' sell me down to Orleans. But I noticed dey wuz a nigger trader roun' de place considable, lately, en I begin to git oneasy. Well, one night I creeps to de do', pooty late, en de do' warn't quite shet, en I hear ole missus tell de widder she gwyne to sell me down to Orleans, but she didn' want to, but she could git eight hund'd dollars for me, en it 'uz sich a big stack o' money she couldn' resis'" (69).

What is a person's word or trust supposed to mean? In the slave-holding South of this novel, not much, especially when it involved money. What is also clear here is that Jim is not the image of the happy, oblivious darkey who is completely unaware of his situation. He shows the audience that he is a man of action when the timing requires it. He tells Huck, "I never waited to hear de res'. I lit out mighty quick, I tell you" (69). If Jim were to represent the happy darkey, he would quietly accept his fate, as does Stowe's Uncle Tom. Jim, however, represents the southern slave more realistically, biding his time and running when propitious. And so it is here that Jim's epic journey toward freedom begins. He alone makes the decision to run, and he is alone when he escapes to Jackson's Island.

Adventures of Huckleberry Finn works as a literary narrative because Twain portrays sharply defined characters who merit the reader's acknowledgment and respect—not shame and embarrassment. Both combine to create for the reader an accessible path into the slaveholding South. Twain extends his images, illustrations, and gallery of characters to provide commentary on two different time periods—the pre–Civil War 1840s and the Reconstruction and post-Reconstruction of the 1870s and 1880s.

In addition, Twain also gives voice and visibility to the twentieth-century African Americans' struggle with our own and society's acknowledgment of who and what we are. Twain seeks to change his reader profoundly, and he does. Would it be too unlikely an assertion, then, to propose that *Adventures of Huckleberry Finn* has a place alongside works like Ralph Ellison's *Invisible Man*, George Schuyler's *Black No More* and *Black Empire*, Wright's *Native Son*, Walker's *The Color Purple*, Morrison's *Song of Solomon*, *Tar Baby*, and *Beloved*? Affected by writers such as Mark Twain, these writers and their works define for readers in the latter part of the twentieth century the racial and cultural wounds that were not cauterized through substantial dialogue but rather were being exacerbated by increasing desires for isolation and intolerance. To this purpose of fiction, Fishkin adds that "novelists, like surgeons, cut straight to the heart. But unlike surgeons, they don't sew up the wound. They leave it open to heal or fester, depending on the septic level of the reader's own environment" (*Lighting Out* 123). Such an assertion for *Adventures of Huckleberry Finn* is not far-fetched. Twain consciously leaves the wound of racism open at the conclusion of this novel, not to diminish Jim but to awaken Huck and the reader to the continuing injustice and contradictions of post-Reconstruction. What Twain did not foresee—but Ellison and the others did—was that Jim would become the emblematic source of the agitation that Twain so ardently sought to address and redress.

Because the wound is yet open or because of unconscious denial, a significant number of African Americans today do not wish to confront and explore the issues and language Twain depicts. Unfortunately, many have deemed the work racist and unworthy to be read not just by themselves but by anyone.[9] This predisposition to preclude critical thinking is rather reminiscent of Pap's telling Huck that because he, Pap, cannot read, Huck will not read.

What we see here is a survival strategy. In an effort to protect themselves and our African American children from any type of intellectual or social discomfort or inquiry, opponents of the novel have donned the mask of nonrecognition of Jim and other African American characters; the motive is ambivalent denial of a history and an important, *undeniable* ancestry. Simply put, if we elect not to recognize the presence and voice of Jim, how can we be expected to identify with him, much less learn from him? If we will not even acknowledge and validate Jim, then how can we be associated with or claim knowledge of that from which we seek separation, or difference? In other words, we as African Americans must first acknowledge the historicity of what Twain depicts before we can claim our difference and separation or exclusion. Failure to recognize the African American presences in this novel places us in the position of appearing to deny a significant portion of our part in the fabric of American history—whether our ancestors were slaves or born free. We cannot afford this luxury. The issue of slavery, of having a biologically and psychologically traceable lineage, of having pride in one's self, culture, and personal worth, are still in a state of becoming in the African American community throughout the United States. While many African Americans, such as my family and I, embrace their slave heritage and see in it admirable strength, resoluteness, and a strong ethic, others prefer to look past this Middle Passage and construct another homeland, Africa, a mythical place of only kings and queens and great civilizations—devoid of its own slave system, and devoid of reality.

You Can't Learn a Nigger to Argue

Verbal Battles

Misconceptions surround Jim in current public discussions. Sometimes the novel is simply not read; at other times it has not been read carefully enough. Various movie versions of Jim fail to render him as the complete, three-dimensional character Twain develops in the novel. Unfortunately, these films provide all that many know of Jim, even though they distort his character and his intent. Before considering Twain's accomplishments in the book, it is helpful to consider the ways in which the movies fail. I will argue in this chapter that Jim, when viewed in the context of classical rhetoric, proves to be an important and profound agent of social change. Hollywood, like some of the novel's academic critics, has not understood the Menippean satire in which Twain envelopes Jim, and lacking the classical perspective, all too easily misread him at crucial moments.

None of the producers and directors of the movies derived from *Adventures of Huckleberry Finn* have remained true to Twain's words, scenes, or language. In the most nostalgic version, a seemingly sincere and puckish Huck, played by Mickey Rooney, reveals clearly that he helps Jim escape only out of fear for his life because of Pap Finn. Quite unlike Twain's presentation of Huck and Jim, this 1939 version lacks the tenacity, the linguistic mastery, and the deliberate presence the novel brings to the relationship between the reluctant abolitionist and the runaway. The movie's Jim, for example, already has a wife and a child in a free state; Jim, consequently, seeks only to join them, rather than buy or *steal* them. The movie blunts even this pretension because Jim's wife and "one" child, misnamed Little Joey, have already purchased their freedom. Slavery from this egregiously softened perspective assumes an unrealistically benevolent, even sanitized and reasonable, quality. In the Mickey Rooney version, no verbal battles occur between Huck and Jim, no chastising of Huck, no apology to Jim. There *is* a scene in which Jim must apologize to Huck for deliberately misleading him with regard to the death of Pap Finn. While the novel attributes Jim's actions to his genuine concern and his desire to shield Huck, the film portrays him as consciously misusing Huck to satisfy his own needs. The free professor from the North, the plantation scenes, the slave auction, Tom Sawyer's deception, the escape, the capture, and the dark conclusion are all missing from the movie. No hint of the failure of Reconstruction and post-Reconstruction emerges. These glaring omissions, by leaving out any contrast between urgings to freedom and the grotesqueness of slavery, further oversimplify the way Jim and the other slaves are characterized. Jim establishes no distinctive voice and visibility. Jim makes no decisive articulation symbolic of what freedom really means, such as his "trash" speech to Huck on the raft. The same significant neutering of Jim emerges in subsequent movies.

A fair question, of course, is "So what?" Does such a substantial difference exist in the movie versions that the essence of Twain's message loses its power and transformative ability? The answer is emphatically, yes. In effect, by revising, deleting, collapsing, creating, and merging scenes—some completely out of sequence or others never introduced at all—moviemakers are acting as social censors, reinforcing reductive stereotypes. In an industry that asserts its own right to free speech, this is a terrible irony. The film portrayals of Jim legitimize the very stereotype of the nineteenth-century slave that Twain's focused portrait so consciously reversed. The dignity and struggle of every slave is reduced to inane humor. Jim remains unvoiced and invisible and, hence, unempowered. Perhaps most disheartening, in the 1960 MGM version of the novel Jim assumes the role of an African King in a circus sideshow, an episode wholly created by Hollywood. Huck, "speaking African," acts as interpreter between Jim and the circus owner and audience. The 1993 Disney version also characterizes Jim as an African warrior. Emerging from the woods in costume, he is not dressed as Twain describes him in the novel's disguise episode; he is outfitted as nothing more than a pawn for the king and duke. When Jim appears, Huck laughs at him as would the viewing audience.

"Shoo fly. Funny, huh? Very funny."

"What in hell's bells are you supposed to be?"

"The king said I was a Swahili warrior. Even taught me some Swahili. Or what he said was Swahili. Sounded like a pig in heat to me."

Later, as the king and duke present themselves to the Wilks daughters, Jim is introduced as an African, captured during a safari like an animal, "who makes a great slave." Jim and the duke engage in unintelligible gibbering grunts and signs. Where Twain reduced his two heroes to satirize our naive expectations, Disney's reproduction transforms them into mere buffoons.

Such overwhelming manipulation of the original subject matter disrupts beyond repair the delicate balance Twain establishes in the novel, a balance between Jim's revelation of himself and Huck's decreasing ambivalence and increasing awareness. When Jim, for example, teaches Huck the value of loyalty, the price of freedom, the importance of family and friends, and the significance of conversation and reevaluation, Twain is endeavoring to make Huck and the audience acutely aware of the magnitude of not just Jim, specifically, but of the southern slave. This objective is waylaid in the movies, which degrade Huck and Jim's dynamic dialogue into comic patter and "gee whiz!" dramatizations. Pivotal scenes, such as the discussions between Jim and Huck on Solomon, family, language, freedom, and friendship, are abandoned in these (re)visionings of Twain's actual text. Hollywood allows a broad license to the term *adaptation*, and the "adapted" films of *Adventures of Huckleberry Finn* contribute, in part, to modern misinterpretations of Twain's Jim.

Like the movie producers and directors, many of Twain's modern opponents do not take into account what Twain as writer is trying to do rhetorically, how he goes about constructing the complex character of Jim. One important device he uses is humor, which serves as an anchor to explore serious and sensitive issues, thereby creating a type of American satire that contains many of the traits found in works by classical satirists. Adapting the styles and themes of earlier satirists such as Juvenal, Horatio, Swift, and Rabelais to the American backwoods setting, Twain paves the way for future American satirists, including those of color such as George Schuyler.[1] Twain essentially created an innovative form of satire by merging classical stylistic satire with regional realism. Oddly enough, some of the more classical traits have caused the greatest agitation in the African American audience: the burlesquing, the exaggeration, the extensive use of verbal and situational irony, the logomachies (or verbal battles), the symbolic reversals, the appearance of carelessness, the symposium setting, the redefining of familiar words, and the use of dialect itself. It is with these classical elements, however, that Twain's narrative literally transcends race and gender as well as time and place.

Looking at what Twain is accomplishing from a rhetorical perspective is important here. Northrop Frye in *Anatomy of Criticism* usefully describes classical satire and its purpose. Frye helps us understand the rhetorical purpose of modern satire by basing his perspective on its classical practitioners—Menippus, Lucian, Varro, and Petronius—and its later neoclassical adaptions by Rabelais, Swift, and Voltaire. "The Menippean satire deals less with people as people as such than with *mental attitudes*. Pedants, bigots, cranks, parvenus, virtuosi, enthusiasts, rapacious and incompetent professional men of all kinds, are handled in terms of their occupational approach to life as distinct from their social behavior. The Menippean satire . . . presents people as *mouthpieces for the ideas they represent*" (309; italics added). We can almost intuitively see how such a quality, when mixed with American literary realism, might confuse inattentive or inexpert readers.

Under Twain's manipulation Menippean representations of mental attitudes include the ways Huck, Jim, and some other characters, relate within a slave-holding society. The audience must identify not only with their occupational personas but also with their social ones. Twain expects the audience to experience as types Miss Watson, the widow, and Aunt Sally, Huck's arbiters of social decorum and religious health as well as the arbiters of the ethics of slavery. Pap Finn is another type: the self-proclaimed patriotic racist and champion of inherited illiteracy. The free African American professor from the North, although based on an actual person, is an important rhetorical counterpoint for Jim at least in part because his role *is* reduced from historical realism to that of a type, identified in the speech of the xenophobic antagonist. Tom Sawyer, the Romantic's romantic and the passive slavery supporter, is the ultimate application of this Menippean type-casting, and his voice is all the more paradoxical to readers who do not realize they can reject him for this reason. The duke and king in their trickster roles quintessentially represent America's sometimes extreme fascination and gullibility with anything remotely symbolizing erudition and class. The Grangerfords, Shepherdsons, and Colonel Sherburn represent the South's finest progenitors of slavery, revealing the cruelty and horror of unchecked inhumanity. The feuding families and Sherburn force the reader to attempt to reconcile such irrational blood lust with rote adherence to mythic southern codes of gentility and Christian behavior. Even this brief a catalog of characters suggests that they are types of the region as much as they are fictional portraits.

All these characters find their way into Huck's consciousness and, finally, his conscience. Huck Finn is the adolescent, the teenager from the other side of the tracks, or river, who at first relies on the rules and regulations of what the Widow Douglas and Miss Watson have taught. Even though Huck experiences typical adolescent tension with these arbiters of morality and behavior, when Jim's flight threatens this world's values, with which he is so familiar, Huck falls back on the lessons and rules learned. It is this tension between an apparently safe, stable, and trustworthy world and a chaotic, illogical, and brutal, even murderous, one that Huck must confront. Jim is a crucial element in this confrontation. Contrary to "static" notions of the slave, Jim, from the moment of their encounter on Jackson's Island, influences and then consciously seeks to agitate and move Huck Finn, a fact revealed in his dialogue and sense of timing in delivery. Primarily, Jim presents himself to Huck as a walking, talking, independent contradiction of what Huck has believed as indisputable truths. Jim is human; Jim is not Huck's intellectual inferior; Jim does have great capacity to love, to be responsible, to dare the odds, and to exercise personal choice.

Through Jim, the reader and Huck cannot ignore the presence of other slave communities and individuals: Jack on the Grangerford plantation, the observant yet careful group of young slaves juxtaposed to the lynch mob; the Wilks's slave family; the slaves on the Phelps's plantation. Peripheral in their placement in the novel, these slaves further solidify who and what Jim represents. They provide an extra layer of authority and proof while also functioning as a series of gauges by which we can follow Huck Finn's transformation. As Huck meets and experiences these individuals, so too must the reader.

With Jim then lies the "Jim dilemma" as the novel unfolds, and with Jim will it remain for some time to come. To resolve this dilemma of individualism within control (Jim) and personal growth (Huck), I propose to look at the college professor as an important symbol, then to explore how slave Jim must act in the opposite way from this free "nigger" and does so through verbal satire created by Twain. Many readers of this novel pay little or no attention to other African American presences Twain renders, including the professor from the North, the "nigger: whom Pap feels should be put up at auction and sold (50). This lack of validation and recognition with regard to the professor's presence is significant, particularly because he anticipates what the Reverend Dr. Martin Luther King describes as the model future leader for African Americans: "[W]e must . . . develop intelligent, courageous and dedicated leadership. . . . In this period of transition and growing social change, there is a dire need for leaders who are calm and yet positive, leaders who avoid the extremes of hot-headedness and Uncle Tomism" (26). When I have asked African American opponents to this novel what they think about the free professor from the North, most recall nothing. They either do not remember him or fail to see his significance to the narrative, just as they overlook the significance of the other slaves on the plantations along the Mississippi.

In the first section of the novel, Twain accomplishes several objectives: he introduces the audience to the two primary characters, Huck and Jim, and he shows that each has been conditioned to believe that he could not be more socially and culturally different than the other. The difference is understood as the South perceived difference. Yet these two are becoming, as the novel progresses, more alike. Twain also introduces the central problems being worked out through the actions, reactions, and dialogue of these two characters: slavery, emancipation, and societal responsibility. And in Chapter Six Twain even introduces the element of the free African American through the diatribe of Pap Finn.

Twain entitles Chapter Six "He Went for Judge Thatcher—Huck Decided to Leave—Political Economy—Thrashing Around." But it could just as easily have been appropriately titled "Any Negro Living Well, Or 'Call This a Govment?' " Although the readers and Huck are consciously aware of Jim, his motivation for running, and the subsequent dilemma this decision causes for Huck, Twain's portrayal of a northern African American in this chapter provides a subliminal, or subconscious, memory tag that remains with us for this first portion of the novel. Once made aware of the other kind of African American, no one—not the audience, Huck, or Pap—can forget the contrasting images between Jim and the professor. Such a juxtaposition provides a tangible, undeniable alternative to slavery. And who better to describe this man than the quintessential racist, Pap Finn himself:

Oh, yes, this is a wonderful govment, wonderful. Why, looky here. There was a free nigger there, from Ohio; a mulatter, most as white as a white man. He had the whitest shirt on you ever see, too, and the shiniest hat; and there ain't a man in that town that's got as fine clothes as what he had; and he had a gold watch and chain, and a silver-headed cane—the awfulest old gray-headed nabob in the State. And what do you think? they said he was a p'fessor in a college, and could talk all kinds of languages, and knowed everything. And that ain't the wust. They said he could *vote*, when he was at home. Well, that let me out. Thinks I, what is the country a-coming to? It was 'lection day, and I was just about to go and *vote*, myself, if I warn't too drunk to get there; but when they told me there was a State in this country where they'd let that nigger vote, I drawed out. I says I'll never vote agin. Them's the very words I said; they all heard me; . . . And to see the cool way of that nigger— why, he wouldn't a give me the road if I hadn't shoved him out o' the way. I says to the people, why ain't this nigger put up at auction and sold?—that's what I want to know. . . . Why, they said he couldn't be sold till he'd been in the State six months, and he hadn't been there that long yet. (49–50)

I have often asked students to explain to me if, as his critics assert, Twain is a racist writing a racist novel, would he render such a bigot as Pap or show an elevated Negro—the professor walking so blatantly and deliberately down the main street? The intensity of Pap Finn's blatant hatred and horrific racist dialogue reveals the import of the professor's intellectual acumen, not to mention his voting rights. Why does Twain reveal that character through the hatred of a racist? Why does Twain show an aggressive, yet nonviolent, response to an irate Pap Finn when the professor refuses to yield the right-of-way just because Pap is white. The student response, regardless of race, is always the same. If they were free-born or freed African Americans, they would not have even thought about going into the South, much less walking so visibly down a main street. Students from Texas to Connecticut to California represent the thousands to whom I have lectured and to whom I have listened. They come from a variety of socioeconomic backgrounds with varied cultural experiences and varied academic levels and placements, yet the majority of them espouse the same views about this. They further deduce that given Pap's depiction of the professor and the psychological effects such a man's presence would have on slaves who would see him, not only is the scene not racist but it is in fact racially uplifting and threatening to the stability of slavery. In many ways the scene with the professor symbolizes the American ideal of life, liberty, and the pursuit of happiness.

Twain provides the reader with this encounter, an image and effect lasting throughout the novel. In contrast to Jim when he wears his mask of subserviency, the professor represents the highest level of intelligence and commands and demands the respect and attention of resistant southerners. While, as some readers contend, the professor does not receive respect from Pap Finn, he accomplishes something far more valuable—undeniable visibility. The professor is not leaving; he is not running; he is not mute. Proponents of slavery may indeed want him to be remanded into slavery, but they cannot act on their desires. The professor keeps the right-of-way in the street—without flinching, according to Pap. Such acts are impossible, even unimaginable, to slaves such as Jim. Equally important, too, is that the professor refuses to descend to Pap Finn's level when Pap pushes him out of the way. He meets Pap's aggression with a resolute presence, what Pap calls his "cool way." He conducted himself in a manner later perfected by the likes of the Reverend Dr. Martin Luther King, Jr.

So what are we to do with this very positive image given to us through the mouth of a self-professed racist? Without such a figure the novel would not necessarily have been compromised; Twain does include him, however, and by doing so acknowledges the presence and the voice and power of the African American who is free. The professor speaks only indirectly through Pap, but this indirect discourse is perhaps the most effective. Having to learn of the professor from such an avowed racist, we learn that in spite of himself the bigot listened and was affected by the encounter. Although we do not actually hear dialogue from the professor, we hear and see him in the vivid descriptions of his literal appearance and his conversations.

As Pap retells this "adventure" to Huck, the event is logged and stored in our minds. For the modern reader, the event must first be explored, for many Americans today are unaware of the statutes and laws regarding a free African American's access to the South. The regulations to which Pap refers are impositions that a contemporary nineteenth-century audience would have known. Specifically, the text alludes to the Missouri Code of 1825, which stated that no African American, even with proof of freedom, could remain in the state longer than six months. By 1847 a revised version of this law read, "No free negro or mulatto shall, under any pretext, emigrate to the State from any other State or territory" (Hughes, Meltzer, and Lincoln 46-48). Twain effectively conveys through Pap the level of anxiety white southerners felt when free African Americans came not only into their midst but into the presence of the slaves themselves. One Virginia lawmaker summed up the sentiment rather well in the *Mirror of Liberty*: "If blacks see all of their color as slaves, it will seem to them a disposition of Providence, and they will be content. But if they see others like themselves free, and enjoying rights they are deprived of, they will repine" (January 1839).[2] What the professor represents can only be aspired to by Jim. The coming Menippean verbal battles will sustain that aspiration in satire.

Jim is undoubtedly a focal point of the novel. Scholars such as Bernard Bell, Charles H. Nilon, Leo Marx, and Rhett S. Jones have all cited Twain's depiction of Jim—what they perceive as Twain's duplicitous depiction of Jim, especially in light of the novel's conclusion—as the primary problem with the novel's continuing effect. Steven Mailloux asserts that Twain's so-called error lies in the novel's overall structure, a structure that weakens and subverts its two primary characters. I propose, however, that neither Twain's depiction of Jim nor the narrative structure subverts the novel's theme, but each serves to strengthen it in several ways.

To accomplish the psychological (re)construction in Huck and the reader, Twain creates a realistic world within a fictional milieu that not only invades Huck Finn's personal space but also displaces the reading audience with its inversions. For example, when Jim elects his moment to run, the timing amplifies the exposure of Miss Watson as a "kindly, greedy" person, in Menippean terms. That Huck becomes, reluctantly at first, Jim's passport provides another example. Their going south in order to go north and Jim's assuming the persona of a runaway while he is in fact a runaway typify the stylistic reversal of audience expectations in classical satire. In the most thought-provoking reversal, Jim is freed on several levels at different times.

The novel's satiric structure seeks consciously to redirect readers' expectations from those of a more photographic novelistic form. Twain submerges the reader deeply into a narrative that is simultaneously literal and symbolic. The result is to create an atmosphere conducive to critical thinking and discussion—not, however, by deception and minimalization of character. His use of satire, specifically the four verbal battles I will discuss in the next few pages, is a deliberate device enabling readers to understand, recognize, and validate the situations, the characters, and the novel's theme. And it is in terms of classical rhetoric that these can be most clearly understood.

For the twentieth-century reader, the novel's focus on the nineteenth century demands that the social concerns of freedom, free will, the rights of the individual, and honor be revisited. A passive or superficial reading of such a work necessarily results in mistakes in interpretation and injured sensibilities. Readers who do not meet the challenge of the work and do not engage in an active reading of the verbal battles, Pap's diatribes, the symposia on slavery and mob mentality, and, finally, the burlesqued and parodic conclusion might well conclude that the novel *is* flawed.

Of the criticisms of the novel, the most pervasively wrong is that, though epic in its construction of southern milieu and of Jim and Huck themselves, the novel ultimately fails in its faulty exchanges between Huck and Jim as well as in its harsh parody at Jim's expense in the concluding twelve chapters. To the contrary, I contend that these exchanges are the very structural means by which Twain initiates his reader into Jim's innermost being. Such verbal battles, or logomachies, are essential traits of most effective satires.[3]

Gary Saul Morson, in his essay "Parody, History, and Metaparody," discusses the purpose and agency of parody, and thus logomachy, which, he writes, targets both social and artistic "environments." That is, it focuses irony on both the pretension of artists and the conventional responses of audiences (Morson and Emerson 63). "Literary parody is . . . a special form of a more general communicative possibility . . ." (63). Citing Bakhtin, Morson continues,

"[P]arody and stylization are types of . . . 'double-voiced words,' or utterances that are designed to be interpreted as the expression of two speakers. . . . The audience of the double-voiced word is therefore meant to hear both a version of the original utterance as the embodiment of its speaker's point of view *and* the second speaker's evaluation of that utterance from a different point of view (65). Every verbal engagement functions as a lens through which the reader observes each participant struggling to understand ideas and beliefs to which he feels innately committed.

Examined as a whole the logomachies in *Adventures of Huckleberry Finn* culminate in an extensive examination of social issues that concerned both the pre–Civil War and post-Reconstruction South: the real meaning of freedom for the freedman, the meaning of wisdom, loyalty, respect, independence, and family. The verbal battles between Huck and Jim, and later between Jim and Tom, enable Twain's reading audiences to see what Menippean satire seeks to expose—the "diseased intellect" resulting from evil and absurdity, in this case the evil and absurdity of the slavery system, class hierarchy, and religious and filial hypocrisy (Frye 309). Rather than being minstrel show failures, in fact, they are some of the novel's most satiric interracial interchanges.

Early in the novel Jim foreshadows his later inarguable logic when he explains to Huck that he has become a runaway. More specifically, he describes to Huck how he determined his mode of escape: "Well, when it come dark I tuck out up de river road, en went 'bout two mile er more to whah dey warn't no houses. I'd made up my mine 'bout what I's agwyne to do. You see ef I kep' on tryin' to git away afoot, de dogs 'ud track me; ef I stole a skift to cross over, dey'd miss dat skift, you see, en dey'd know 'bout whah I lan' on de yuther side en whah to pick up my track. So I says, a raff is what I's arter; it doan' *make* no track" (69–70). In a special way, it is Jim's need, not Huck's, that establishes the basis for the most important symbol of the novel. The verbal battles that come later in the novel are each syllogistic expansions of the logic Jim patterns here.

There are four major logomachies in *Adventures of Huckleberry Finn*: (1) the discussion about securing the canoe; (2) the discussion on King Solomon; (3) the discussion about language; and (4) the discussion of incarcerating snakes with Jim. The second and third of these verbal battles occur between Huck and Jim as they journey down the Mississippi in Chapter 9 and Chapter 14. While the majority of critics concur that Jim wins each of these arguments, the rhetorical strategy by which he wins has not received much attention.[4]

An important consideration is the context in which the logomachies occur. Take, for example, the episode where Huck and Jim board the wreck. Huck, using the information that he himself has gotten from Tom Sawyer, initiates and defines for "ignorant" Jim what an adventure is. In doing so, Huck puts Jim in the role he himself has held in relation to Tom Sawyer, thus creating a second level of satiric role-playing. Later back in the raft, Huck, explains to Jim what has been happening to them—they have just experienced an adventure (109). Just as Huck has been student to Tom's instruction, so now Huck becomes teacher and Jim, learner. Jim, however, quickly and masterfully gains control, thereby reversing the roles in their relationship. By assertively declaring that "he didn't want no more adventures" (109), he counters and transforms Huck's concept and definition, shifting the focus of the adventure so that it signals the beginning of his escape to freedom. His refocusing functions as a syllogistic agency, or, in other words, a logical stance with which Huck can find no error in rationality: "he judged it was all up with *him*, anyway it could be fixed; for if he didn't get saved he would get drownded; and if he did get saved, whoever saved him would send him back home so as to get the reward, and then Miss Watson would sell him South, sure" (109).[5] Jim's reasoning here is totally logical. In a society that earnestly believes in choices, Jim surmises that he has none. Without some *deus ex machina*, his chances are at this point like those of many slaves who tried to run away and were caught and sent back to a far worse situation than they had left.[6]

After listening to Jim's rationale Huck must acknowledge Jim's intelligence and determines that Jim "was most always right; he had an uncommon level head, for a nigger" (109). Such inescapable logic from Jim to Huck makes Jim, then, one to whom Huck will listen, at least as much as a "nigger" needs to be listened to. Note that here Huck feels the necessity to qualify his praise of Jim. The qualifier is framed into the sentence as an important consideration, yet Twain places it structurally so that the real meaning of the sentence is not dependent on this additional comment. The thematic result of such syntactical manipulation is a specifically adjusted understanding of Huck's acknowledgment of Jim's intellectual power. So begins Huck's transformative journey. Threatened by the arguments, he reveals his dilemma that such cannot be the case because Jim is, after all, a "nigger."

At this point every action is for all or nothing in Jim's mind. For the runaway slave, once committed to running, the reality of being caught and dealt with severely tempered the eager anticipation of eventual freedom with the immediate fear of retribution. Turning back to slavery or expecting to find an empathetic ear and heart at the ready were not realities of the time. The slave catcher, and sometimes the African American informant, waited patiently but determinedly at every junction of the road to freedom. Caution, keen observation, and a strong dose of common sense were the runaway's watch words. The raft voyage will embody these virtues. In the next seventeen chapters Jim will be at his most clear-cut. Within Huck's mind, these astringent experiences will realize his earlier description of good eating as opposed to the food at Miss Watson's. Life in this barrel of odds and ends will "get mixed up, and the juice kind of swaps around, and the things go better" (18). Everything for Huck will indeed be mixed up and swapped around because the slave's purpose conflicts with an urge to adventures which does not always lead to such a clear and smooth assessment. Being with Jim causes Huck to begin a process of questioning what he has been taught. What he is presently empirically seeing, hearing, and feeling merges with a higher purpose. Huck will redefine just what "better" means in life as in food, a redefining that will have substantial effects on him and, Twain hopes, the reader.

Huck still views himself as superior to Jim because of his skin color, an important point. Abstractly, however, Jim begins what Burke terms a mode of transcendence (*Rhetoric of Motives*). Jim appropriates the slave stereotype whenever necessary and appears to acknowledge his "oppressor" in order to maintain the voice he has already established. If his escape to freedom is to be successful, he must seem to acknowledge the slave-to-master relationship, even with a boy like Huck, and even more so with Tom later, though as a slave in the South what he desires most is deliberately antithetical to what the white southerner seeks. Twain alludes to having witnessed this kind of behavior on the part of slaves in his *Autobiography*. On remembering the slaves of his boyhood, he states that those slaves who may have disagreed with the institution itself wisely said nothing of their displeasure or desire to be free because of the consequences. (*Autobiography* 6-7)

Jim's aggressive logic, however, confronts Huck in the first verbal exchange. In the Solomon logomachy, we see for the first time Jim's double-voicing.[7] This unique and coded form of communication is perhaps best defined by seeing Frances Harper's rendering of it in *Iola Leroy, Or Shadows Uplifted* (1893). One of the more humorous of the many examples Harper's novel provides of double-voicing involves a kitchen slave and her interpretation of her mistress's evaluation of the tide of the war, which is decidedly going against the South:

"Anyhow, Bobby, things goes mighty contrary in dis house. Ole Miss is in de parlor prayin' fro de Secesh to gain de day, and we's prayin' in de cabins and kitches for de Yankees to get de bes' ob it. . . .

"She said when dey com'd down yere she wanted all de men to hide, for dey'd kill all de men, but dey wouldn't tech de women."

"It's no such thing. She's put it all wrong. Why them Yankees are our best friends."

"Dat's jis' what I thinks. Ole Miss was jis' tryin to skeer a body. An' when she war done she jis' set down and sniffled an' cried, an' I war so glad I didn't know what to do. But I had to hole in. An' I made out I war orfulo sorry. An' Jinny said, 'O Miss Nancy, I hope dey won't come yere.' An' she said, 'I'se jis' 'fraid dey will come down yere and gobble up eberything dey can lay dere hands on'. . . . An' when she war gone, we jis' broke loose. Jake turned somersets, and said he warn't 'fraid ob dem Yankees; he know'd which side his brad was buttered on. . . . An' I jis' had to put my han' ober her [Jinny's] mouf to keep ole Miss from yereing her. Oh, but we hab a good time" (10-11).

Such double-voicing may include the slave's feigning forgetfulness, ignorance of an issue, surprise, sadness, or even humor where there really is none. The southern white hears one thing while the slaves hear something different. The double-voicing can communicate within the slave community, or it can create another level of ironic meaning and comic confusion when the audience is the white who held to the philosophy of slavery. Jim, for example, humorously signifies on Huck's own topic when he tells him that he has simply "forgotten" the definition of harem but that he now remembers it:

"But mostly they [kings] hang round the harem."

"Roun' de which?"

"Harem."

"What's de harem?"

"The place where he [king] keep his wives. Don't you know about the harem? Solomon had one; he had about a million wives."

"Why, yes, dat's so; I—I'd done forgot it. A harem's a bo'd'n-house, I reck'n. Mos' likely dey has rackety times in de nussery. En I reck'n de wives quarrels considable; en dat 'crease de racket." (111)

Like most people engaged in argument, each wants to win. When confronted, however, by an unfamiliar word, Jim admits his weakness and inquires of Huck what it means. When Jim then counters with the assertion to temporary forgetfulness, he employs a rhetorical strategy. Now that he has remembered, he must do more with the word if he wishes to win the argument. In winning, he establishes his voice as well as his localized pragmatic viewpoint.

Jim elaborates the definition so as to make it his own. His position is based on his role as a man and as a parent. Having come to trust and depend on Huck's sense of humanity despite his social conditioning, Jim speaks directly to Huck, fully expecting him to listen and learn and respond accordingly. Essentially, he speaks as an individual, a visible, worthwhile person speaking to an adolescent who honestly believes in the inherent ignorance of Jim's entire race. What makes Jim's signification important is how he does it. The harem for Jim becomes a "bo'd'n-house" with "rackety times in de nussery." The best part of the joke lies in symbolizing a family place as a boarding house which, had Solomon any real wisdom, could be converted into a more useful building—a "biler-factry." Jim transforms the idea of "harem" from a place of polygamy, concubines, and female servants for male-focused sexual gratification and redefines it to communicate his sincere and constant love of family and home. He changes the nature, function, and focus of the harem, reflecting his own, personal values. Huck, possibly unaware of this rhetorical turning, is like the reader swept along in Jim's encoding and confounding of ancient history with the language of modern life. Jim, through his use of language, foreshadows his difference from Huck's human stereotype which will later become central in the novel. As they continue their journey, Jim will use this skill to motivate and sustain Huck's changing perspective.

Writers and critics such as Zora Neale Hurston, Henry Louis Gates, Jr., and Roger Abrahams have written of the ethnic difference the southern slave brings to standard English: "language of blackness encodes and names its sense of independence through a rhetorical process that we might think of as Signifyin(g) black difference. . . [which can] reverse or undermine pretense or even one's opinion about one's own status. The use of repetition and reversal (chiasmas) constitutes an implicit parody of a subject's own complicity in illusion" (Gates, *The Signifying Monkey* 289). Based on Gates's assertion then, as Jim begins to transcend his slave role, he acquires and projects a stronger language. He does not attempt to appropriate and identify with his southern white representative, Huck, and he thus does not lose or compromise his own unique voice. An abstract definition that applies to Jim appears in Burke: "The Negro does not become equal to the white by a kind of intellectual 'passing.' He can recognize that his particular act must be adapted to the nature of his historical situation in which he happens to be placed; yet at the same time, he can view this situation universally (thereby attaining the kind of transcendence at which all men aim, and at which the Negro spiritual had aimed, though there the aim was at the spiritual transcending of a predestined material slavery" (*Rhetoric of Motives* 195). When viewed in this linguistic frame, Huck's discussion now becomes a verbal as well as a psychological battle because Jim asserts an antithetical view regarding Solomon's renowned wisdom: "Yit dey say Sollermun de wises' man dat ever live'. I doan' take no stock in dat. Bekase why: would a wise man want to live in de mids' er sich blimblammin' all de time? No—'deed he wouldn't" (111). Jim is not trying to pass as a white intellectual, but he is striving for a type of verbal and critical equality. Jim gains his intellectual equality not by pretending to be something that he is not or speaking in ways that are unfamiliar; he uses and relies on his own knowledge and mastery of the language as he commands it.

Readers must acknowledge what Jim is saying on the surface as well as below it in order to comprehend fully the deliberate language manipulation. The doubleness is particularly important with an African American audience.[8] The relationship that emerges with this form of satire attempts to push the reader past the literal level to one that agitates the reader to rethink the occasion that caused the statement or scene. When Jim clearly and assertively says not only that does he not believe in the infallible wisdom of Solomon but that he disagrees with, even does not care about, what the widow has said about Solomon and his superiority, he has transcended the accepted bounds of any living slave in the South and of most freedmen during post-Reconstruction. Overt disapproval or disagreement with the master and the master's symbols was in no way tolerated.[9]

Twain accomplishes through Jim a linguistic realism for African Americans. Critics such as Houston Baker and Robert Burns Stepto contend that African American writers are often successful in enabling their characters to speak in a language of repudiation and authentication. In Baker's *Long Black Song: Essays in Black American Literature and Culture*, he defines repudiation as "characteristic of black American folklore; and this is one of the most important factors in setting black American literature apart from white American literature" (17). Both styles—literal and sub-text expression—focus on the African American speaker taking command—through manipulation, encoding, or double-voicing—over language and the ensuing dialogue. Jim displays this sort of linguistic control. Baker and Stepto are referring specifically to African American writers, but I believe that Twain listened to many African American voices as he developed as a writer, and his rendering of Jim necessarily reflects this exposure.

Jim's other voice uses the actual biblical events, which he redacts, or transforms and amplifies, to communicate his own message. Jim again displays his mastery of redefining and thereby shifting the focus:

"I doan k'yer what de widder say, he *warn't* no wise man, nuther. He had some er de dad-fetchedes' ways I ever see. Does you know 'bout dat chile dat he 'uz gwyne to chop in two?"

"Yes, the widow told me all about it."

". . . You jes' take en look at it a minute. Dah's de stump, dah,—dat's one er de women; heah's you—dat's de yuther one; I's Sollermun; en dish-yer dollar bill's de chile. Bofe un you claims it. What does I do? Does I shin aroun' mongs' de neighbors en fine out which un you de bill *do* b'long to, en han' it over to de right one, all safe en soun', de way dat anybody dat had any gumption would? No—I take en whack de bill in *two*, en give half un it to you, en de yuther half to de yuther woman. . . . Now I want to ast you: what's de use er dat half a bill?. . . En what use is a half a chile?" (111)

This scene accomplishes several objectives of the classic Menippean satire. Simultaneously, it shows use of the double voice.[10] Jim's "signification" causes the reader to rethink the historical status of Solomon and to reconfigure conventional preformed Sunday school ideas. Jim assumes a new status, that of the one who makes the decisions and decrees the fate of those who serve him. By assuming the persona of Solomon and thereby appropriating Solomon's voice and authority, Jim assertively rejects the silence his slave and "nigger" status have imposed upon him (cf. Morrison, *Playing in the Dark* 55-57).

A close reading of the text again reveals Jim's deep feeling for family, children, and responsibility. To him—one whose family can be and is sold away from him and from each other—Solomon's apparent wisdom is interpreted only as the concomitant result of a man's having so much of everything, including wives and children, that slaughtering one would matter little. Jim imprints into Huck's consciousness the significance of loss and the value of family, a point not lost on Huck, as we see later in the novel when he hears Jim moaning and mourning the loss of his family and again when he sees his first slave auction. On this crucial point about family, then, Jim is implacable. When Huck tries to show him the error in his logic, Jim asserts, "Blame de pint! I reck'n I knows what I knows. En mine you, de *real* pint is down furder—it's down deeper. . . .You take a man dat's got on'y one er two chillen; is dat man gwyne to be waseful o' chillen? No, he ain't; he can't 'ford it.

He know how to value 'em" (112). In arguing for family, Jim's aggressiveness again has also broken the conventional boundaries between masters and slaves in the old South.

Following the establishment of the family motif, Huck and Jim's next verbal battle on language repeats the same rhetorical strategy of the first with one significant elaboration: Twain makes Jim's linguistic manipulation more evident to the reader. Huck, agitated that he has "lost" the Solomon argument, decides to change the subject to another topic about which he feels more confident—French kings and the French language. This parody not only satirizes American fascination with royalty but reconstructs Huck's definition of language and perhaps more importantly the way language defines and empowers a man. Jim uses a rhetorical strategy reminiscent of Frederick Douglass's appropriation of persuasive models in *The Columbian Orator* for his own rhetorical style of argumentation. He intently listens and "learns" while Huck arranges his flawless argument. Huck seductively says,

"Looky here, Jim; does a cat talk like we do?"

"No, a cat don't."

"Well, does a cow?"

"No, a cow don't, nuther."

"Does a cat talk like a cow, or a cow talk like a cat?"

"No, dey don't."

"It's natural and right for 'em to talk different from each other, ain't it?"

" 'Course."

"And ain't it natural and right for a cat and a cow to talk different from *us*?"

"Why, mos' sholy it is."

"Well, then, why ain't it natural and right for a *Frenchman* to talk different from us? You answer me that." (113-14)

Huck thinks that he has constructed the perfect, infallible argument—the perfect syllogism. He waits only for Jim to acquiesce and admit defeat. Jim, however, tropes on Huck's own argument by using the very same strategy and constructing against him:[11]

"Is a cat a man, Huck?"

"No."

"Well, den, dey ain't no sense in a cat talkin' like a man. Is a cow a man?—er is a cow a cat?"

"No, she ain't either of them."

"Well, den, she ain' got no business to talk like either one er the yuther of 'em. Is a Frenchman a man?"

"Yes."

"*Well*, den! Dad blame it, why doan' he *talk* like a man? You answer me *dat*!"

I see it warn't no use in wasting words—you can't learn a nigger to argue. So I quit. (114)

Huck "quits" because Jim has "learned" so well that nothing else remains to be said. Huck's *ad hominum* shift is a marker for his defeat and frustration as well as a reminder to the reader of the racist premises on which his regard for Jim has been based.

Significantly, Jim is aware of what he has done and how he has done it. This awareness emerges when he "forgets" himself and continues explaining to Huck just how independent-minded he actually is. When Huck asks Jim what would he think if a person were to say to him, "*Polly-voo-franzy. . . ,*" Jim responds assertively, yet cautiously under the mask and through the voice of the slave: "I wouldn' think nuff'n; I'd take en bust him over de head. Dat is, if he warn't white. I wouldn't 'low no nigger to call me dat" (113). The first statement, compound in structure, is indicative, assertive, and asks permission from no one to maintain voice and, therefore, authority. The second clause is a conditional fragment, independent from and yet dependent on the previous sentence construction—a qualifier after the fact, a readjustment of the mask. The third clause, though independent, also functions as a corollary to the first. Jim's quick and effective structural readjustment regains control of the verbal battle so that Huck cannot see the real man too soon. Through the use of the rhetorical fragment, Jim accomplishes verbal irony by allowing his opponent, Huck, to believe that Jim "gives up" on a specific point. The independent clause that follows functions as a clear, self-reliant certainty. Jim, if left alone, will defend himself just as any man would, regardless of color. What he reveals initially here is just that—regardless of color no man whom he does not understand will insult him. Only after he realizes what he has allowed to escape verbally and internally does he redirect Huck's attention by acknowledging racial difference.

Again and again, Twain places Jim and Huck in these logomachal frames. The value of the novel is that both characters can develop and evolve "naturally" in this rhetorical model. The progressive and organic process of verbal battles arranges and codifies attitudes of the characters toward the struggles of social mores. The reader, too, develops and evolves with these characters. Inculcated beliefs and traditions involving abstract concepts such as racial equality, freedom, family, and language shift. The shifting demands methodical persuasion, but only a subtle satire such as Twain's can depict it without preaching. The reader discovers and experiences a different truth as the characters themselves discover and experience different truths.

In addition to the three logomachies examined here, others occur between Huck and Jim throughout the novel. The most crucial verbal battle occurs in Chapter 15. The early ones have been a prerequisite for making Huck's and the reader's minds ready for change; the later battles are elaborations and amplifications of Jim's character. The pivotal logomachy in Chapter 15 focuses on the final trick Huck plays on Jim while they are in the fog. After Huck has made Jim think that he has died, only to be restored miraculously, Huck then shifts the narrative to make Jim believe that all that has happened in the storm occurred only in Jim's mind. For the audience as well as for Jim such a prank is ethically debilitating. *Adventures of Huckleberry Finn* opponents, especially those who are African American, contend that all the progress and visibility—the sense of presence—Jim has heretofore gained, Huck obliterates. This "joke" calls into question Jim's mental capabilities of comprehending and discerning the difference between the waking and dream worlds. It is crucial, therefore, for Jim, if he is to preserve the identity Twain has established, to be assertive and focused.

In his handling of this scene Twain displays a rhetorical device called an antistrephon—or the turning of an opponent's argument to one's own position—coupled with an additional rhetorical strategy, metastasis—or the taking of an insult and transforming it into a different meaning. Using these strategies, Jim, the man made invisible and mute by slavery, turns the table. Rejecting the constrictions imposed by slavery on language and expression, Jim makes his stand against a dismissive and reductive southern white establishment as he decidedly and clearly chastises Huck Finn. Huck symbolizes the transgressions of his race; in his response to Jim he also represents the redemptive potential of his race. Jim looks at Huck steadily, synecdochally placing Huck in the role of errant child. Twain, however, also makes him serve as a symbol of southern treatment of slaves: "What do dey stan' for? I's gwyne to tell you. When I got all wore out wid work, en wid de callin' for you, en went to sleep, my heart wuz mos' broke bekase you wuz los', en I didn' k'yer no mo' what become er me en de raf'. En when I wake up en fine you back agin', all safe en soun', de tears come en I could a got down on my knees en kiss' yo' foot I's so thankful. En all you wuz thinkin' 'bout wuz how you could make a fool uv ole Jim wid a lie. Dat truck dah is *trash*; en trash is what people is dat puts dirt on de head er dey fren's en makes 'em ashamed" (121). Rather than taking each item of debris and divining its meaning as Huck requests, Jim takes each act of kindness and concern he has shown Huck Finn over the course of their journey and defines for the boy, perhaps for the first time in Huck's life, the meaning of friendship, loyalty, and filial or family responsibility.

In many ways this section is the turning point of the novel. Jim is no longer invisible, and his "silence" is clearly under his control. This decisive encounter signifies the redefining of the slave/master, white/black relationship to one of caretaker-guardian/charge and adult/child, consequently amplifying Jim's manhood. Of equal significance is Huck's realization of this shift in their relationship. To mark the event, Twain has him tell us that he would have to think long and hard before humbling himself not to Jim but to a "nigger": "It was fifteen minutes before I could work myself up to go and humble myself to a nigger—but I done it, and I warn't ever sorry for it afterwards, neither. I didn't do him no more mean tricks, and I wouldn't done that one if I'd a knowed it would make him feel that way" (121).

Many critics fail to see that it is not simply apologizing to Jim that takes Huck the fifteen minutes. Jim is the catalyst for a much larger social (re)conditioning that Huck experiences as a result of this devastating joke. Huck must reorganize and revise what he has been taught with respect to the relationship between slaves and southern whites. Before now, apologizing would never have been a viable option under any circumstances. So when Huck works himself up "to go and humble myself to a *nigger*" (italics mine), his actions are those not of one individual making a single, personal decision; rather, it is a decision that implies necessary societal changes and (re)visionings. As readers, we must not overlook the apparently singular yet really universal impact of this one act. Once Huck apologizes, nothing can ever be the old way it was, not only between these two but also between Huck and any slave.

What Huck has always thought to be true and indisputable about "the slave" undergoes a subtle and profound change in the first third of the novel. The audience, too, undergoes a change: what it thought to be true of the South, the slave, and Mark Twain is not exactly what appears. The nineteenth-century audience was prepared for the social, political, and psychological transformation Huck and the audience undergoes. Twain's African American contemporaries, like Anna Julia Cooper, William Wells Brown, Frederick Douglass, Frances Harper, Pauline Hopkins, and David Ruggles, probably understood exactly what Twain was trying to do. The influence of Twain's style reveals itself in Harper's *Iola Leroy, or Shadows Uplifted*, Hopkins's *Contending Forces, A Romance Illustrative of Negro Life North and South*, and Cooper's *A Voice from the South*.[12]

Unlike Twain's contemporary audience, the twentieth-century reading audience struggles with Twain's rendering of the Jim. Perceptions of the southern slave as timid, docile, and invisible, even though slave escape narratives proved that many were not, permeated the South during the eighteenth and nineteenth centuries (as Stowe's *Uncle Tom's Cabin* demonstrates). These perceptions gained greater prominence, ironically, during the New Negro Movement of the Harlem Renaissance. Activist Marcus Garvey, concurring with Stowe's depiction in 1854 and in 1855 of Uncle Tom, makes an assessment that would inevitably become associated with Jim as well: "The black man has a kind heart and no one knows it more than the white man of the North American continent. We withstood slavery and yet we still smile. It is because our hearts are tuned to righteousness and love. . . . We can always be regarded as a peace-loving people. I feel sure if there is any trouble in any district, *it isn't the Negro. The only trouble the Negro will make is to get drunk*" (qtd. in Moses 17; italics added). This stereotype would haunt generations to come. The "day of 'aunties,' 'uncles' and 'mammies' . . . [of] Uncle Tom and Sambo have passed on . . . ," Alain Locke, in his seminal essay, "The New Negro," would proclaim. His denouncement of the "spectre" of slaves—their experiences, and their language—was taken up by others in the twentieth century: Malcolm X echoed the same sentiments in the early 1960s. While I am not asserting that Locke intended consciously to preclude this important element in American history, his selection of images have had a detrimental effect on the psyche of many twentieth-century African Americans. Locke and others in their quest to have the Negro born anew forgot that no birth can occur without lineage—parents and, in this case, the aunties and uncles and especially the Jims, who did establish their dignity in transition. Again, Harper's *Iola Leroy*, Hopkins's *Contending Forces*, and Zora Neale Hurston's *Their Eyes Were Watching God* as well as some of her short stories represent a few of the many works that rely on having a representative community of seniors who perhaps did not escape slavery but who nonetheless carry the torch of the community: the tales and legends and history of the slave quarters and experience—those enduring individuals who did not revolt.

In the second portion of the novel—the mid-section—Twain extends the parameters of Huck's empirical learning along the Mississippi to include a panorama of people and places. We will be able to ascertain to what degree Huck has learned from Jim the meanings of family, freedom, honor, and friendship by visiting this section of the novel next.

In the Dark, Southern Fashion

Encounters with Society

In an interview with Claudia Tate, Alice Walker says, "If the black community fails to support its own writers, it will never have the knowledge of itself that will make it great. . . . [W]hen we really respect ourselves, our own thoughts, our own words, when we really love ourselves, we won't have any problem whatsoever selling and buying books or anything else" (Walker, *Black Women* 183). Walker becomes empowered to respect herself through imaginative literature, and the middle section of *Adventures of Huckleberry Finn*, although penned by a white author, promotes a similar transformation into self-esteem. In the nineteenth century, Twain's work was significant in that it brought the ideas of African Americans, ideas shared by such writers as Anna Cooper, to a wide audience they could not hope to reach. The transformation that takes place transcends race, both the race of the author and the race of the characters, and, especially for some African American readers, creates a paradox. Reference to other narratives and the idea of the Menippean Symposia will help us to understand this paradox as it appears in the middle of the novel.

As with works such as Miguel Cervantes's *Don Quixote de la Mancha*, Lewis Carroll's *Alice in Wonderland* and *Through the Looking Glass*, and George Schuyler's *Black No More*, *Adventures of Huckleberry Finn*, in its critical midsection, navigates its two central characters toward a recognition of the need for a new "course of action or thought," a course that can ultimately emancipate them "from formulated principles of conduct" (Frye 286-87). Of course, such emancipation also affects the audience. To effect this kind of paradox and transformation, Twain frames his novel in a Menippean symposium, which creates a base for the emergence of a dialectic between two or more characters in which "opinions and ideas and culture interest are expressed and explored. The novelist shows his exuberance either by an exhaustive analysis of human relationships . . . or of social phenomena. . . . Human society is studied in terms of the [society's] intellectual pattern" (Frye 310-11). In *Adventures of Huckleberry Finn* that intellectual pattern is slavery with its concomitant Southern response, ambivalence. Twain places the characters on the mighty Mississippi, the banks of which are peppered with towns and varied townsfolk, all functioning within the same social context—slavery. It is then the journey along the Mississippi and interaction with these towns that create the Menippean structure of the symposium.

Anna Julia Cooper and her nineteenth-century contemporaries viewed their southern brethren as "[f]ull of vitality and natural elasticity, the severest persecution and oppression could not kill them out or even sour their temper" (108). They endured. Should we feel proud because they did so and imprinted on us their hopes for a better racial future? Or should we turn in shame from our ancestors because they never mastered standard English, because they seemed to demur to their oppressors, because they continued in slavery? Wilson Jeremiah Moses, in *Black Messiahs and Uncle Toms*, describes the paradox as "a desire to cling to the myth of moral superiority with which the romantic racialists of the nineteenth century had endowed them [nationalists of the Harlem Renaissance], but counterpoised by the recognition that there was something *degrading about drawing one's self-image from a slavery experience in which one was forced to play submissive roles*" (51; italics added). The pride we should, and do at times, feel in Huck, Jim, the northern professor, Jack, and other characters too often mutates into a form of self-loathing and historical denial, our Jim dilemma.

Moses focuses primarily on the participants in the Harlem Renaissance, such as Marcus Garvey, as originating these negative interpretations, but he also traces such ideas and sentiments back to Martin Delany, Robert Alexander Young, Alexander Crummell, and Edward Wilmot Blyden (Moses 51). The legacy has had a profound effect on modern African Americans—young and mature, student and parent, activist and nonactivist alike. In many instances, unless the southern slave reached the mythic proportions of a Sojourner Truth, Harriet Tubman, or Frederick Douglass, their narratives have been withheld altogether from the high school classroom and only rarely presented in colleges. The prototypes for Jim go unsung: the Uncle Daniels who remained or who ran but suffered torture en route, the Katies who went the way of the Underground Railroad, or the thousand Hannahs who were continuously sold and resold at auction. They died without their freedom but not without their desire and passion for freedom. Sadly and inappropriately, they now are made to appear in the annals of history, including those of modern African Americans, as Uncle Toms or "handkerchief heads,"[1] if they appear at all.

With the interpretive groundwork in place, it is easier to see why *Adventures of Huckleberry Finn* presents African American readers with such a series of dilemmas. The alleged (re)invisibility of Jim creates in the novel's midsection another set of issues for the African American reading audience and others who identify with the "problem" of race. I see Walker's reference to the black community's "own writers" as emblematic of a concentric circle, a circle that includes those non-African Americans who have made sincere efforts to render the voice, presence, and sociohistorical place of any individual or culture on the fringes of society, as Mark Twain did in *Adventures of Huckleberry Finn*. The reader knows Jim through Jim's own reported statements. We experience the professor as related by Pap Finn, the quintessential racist. More importantly, Twain unmutes other slaves in the novel, like Jack, and juxtaposes those voices next to the likes of Pap and the Widow. Yet the falsely weighted negative view of these moments separates us from the characters we are supposed to and need to experience.

As previously noted, the slave narrative was a popular genre, though until recently not much of it was included in the conventional classroom literary canon. Narratives by Douglass, Gustavas Vassa, and Harriet Jacobs, for example, were as popular as Phillis Wheatley's poetry. But many of the African American works, including the African American periodicals, were shrouded in obscurity until the mid- to late twentieth century.[2] In opposition to the neglect of these works, Twain's novel, with its intimate portrayals of blacks, has survived, controversial as it is. For many years, it alone has held the space that only recently has expanded to include the slave narratives and other works of African Americans. Twain's narrative has thus played an important and vital role in recording the African American southern presence. Its chronicle of an important period in American history brings to the reader a realistic and unromanticized voice of the African American slave which stood as successful surrogate for the others for a century.[3] Anna Julia Cooper capitalizes on the image Twain unveils: "With massive brawn and indefatigable endurance they wrought under burning suns and chilling blasts, in swamps and marshes—they cleared the forests, tunneled mountains, threaded the land with railroads, planted, picked, and ginned the cotton, produced the rice and the sugar for the markets of the world. Without money and without price they poured their hearts' blood into the enriching and developing of this country. They wrought but were silent" (179). Far from showing slaves as impotent, an embarrassment, a closed and unremembered footnote to America's history and literary legacy, writers and critics like Twain and Cooper define and assert the slave's visibility and resonance.

The question of the lack of African American presence at the forefront of literature brings us back to Twain, back to the midsection of *Adventures of Huckleberry Finn*. The first section ended with the momentous scene in Chapter 15 in which Jim and Huck confront the real issue of the entire work—what defines a man, an individual. The middle section of the novel, with what critics perceive as Jim's disappearance, creates too much discomfort for many in the African American reading audience. Jane Smiley in her essay, "Say It Ain't So, Huck," for example, takes the position that "[i]t is with the feud that the novel begins to fail, because from here on the episodes are mere distractions from the true subject of the work: Huck's affection for and responsibility to Jim. The signs of failure are everywhere, as Jim is pushed to the side of the narrative, hiding on the raft and confined to it, while Huck follows the duke and the dauphin on shore to the scenes of much simpler and much less philosophically taxing moral dilemmas, such as fraud" (65).

Smiley and other opponents agree that after this point, when Jim makes brief reappearances, he does so only as the burlesqued comic foil to Huck, the duke, and the dauphin. Contrary to this argument is Gladys Carmen Bellamy in "Roads to Freedom." Bellamy asserts that the novel's midsection is where the satire and thematic power of the book rest because it brings "Huck and Jim into contact with the outside world," a world she describes as a "cross-section of the South" (18). However, Bellamy acknowledges only one of Jim's scenes in this section as important, his personal narrative about his children, 'Lizabeth and Johnny, in Chapter 23. Like many of the book's supporters and detractors, she overlooks other equally significant scenes. Our purpose then must be to expand the recognition of the full presence of African Americans in this area of the book, to see how Cooper's vision was realized in Twain's fictional portrayals.

As Huck could not, neither can we simply jump arbitrarily from his discovery of Jim as a regular, visible human being in the novel's first section to his truly profound assertion at the conclusion of the midsection when he decides to continue to protect Jim: "All right, then, I'll *go* to hell" (272). How does Huck come to consciously yield up his soul for his changed belief? To grow with Huck, we must understand his affection and his nineteenth-century sense of loyalty and moral rightness and, more importantly, his unwavering, consistent, indomitable respect for Jim as a human being, a man, a mentor whose voice must ultimately supersede the voices of the widow, Miss Watson, Judge Thatcher, and the whole South. For a real transformation to take place, Huck's allegiance to Jim must develop to the degree that he feels compelled to act. Through powerfully provocative maneuvers, Twain moves us to consider the ways Jim is constantly recruiting Huck's support and solidifying his subsequent transformation, thereby sustaining and expanding Jim's only chance for freedom.

Jim and Huck's approaching Cairo created an imaginative impasse for Twain. In 1876 he ran out of steam and did not resume writing the novel until 1883. Some critics view this period as evidence of a weak point, an admission that Twain did not know what to do or where to go with these characters. Perhaps he should have allowed them to cross over to free soil at Cairo and thus conclude the novel. For Twain, however, the issue was not so simple. For what reason was he writing this book? Had the initial purpose and vision changed? There were new issues about which he had to think. These years were for him profound and metamorphic. He experienced what he perceived as dualism and hypocrisy in American society, shifted his own political affiliation, observed an upheaval in religious order with the Henry Ward Beecher scandal, traveled abroad, and was, as Louis J. Budd says, "increasingly gripped by a passion for the freedman's welfare" (92). Twain even came to realize that some who claimed to be abolitionists were in fact of the "Wretched Freedman who longed for slavery's school of literature" (Foner 258-59). Twain's emerging feelings of opposition to generally "accepted pieties, patriotic, moral, and cultural" found their voices in *Adventures of Huckleberry Finn* (Kaplan, *Mark Twain* 110).

Rejecting the Cairo crossover in the novel allowed Twain to yield himself up to the powers and personalities of his characters, and Jim and Huck are most definitely at this point separate individuals with separate voices and beliefs. Each has his way of making meaning, a way that expanded Twain's own voice. Twain seems to have experienced something like what Alice Walker recalls undergoing during the writing of *The Color Purple*: the voices simply stopped talking. She had to "study to be quiet," so that when the right time appeared, she would be able not only to hear the words but to listen to the message, to the dialectic:

When I was sure the characters of my new novel were trying to form (or, as I invariably thought of it, trying to contact me, to speak *through me*), I began making plans to leave New York. . . . I would be able to write. I was not. . . . So, I gave it up for a year. Whenever I was invited to speak I explained I was taking a year off for Silence. (I also wore an imaginary bracelet on my left arm that spelled the word.) Everyone said, Sure, they understood. . . . There were days and weeks and even months when nothing happened. Nothing whatsoever. I worked on my quilt, took long walks with my lover, lay on an island we discovered in the middle of the river and dabbled my fingers in the water. . . . And, of course, everything was happening. Celie and Shug and Albert were getting to know each other, coming to trust my determination to serve their entry (sometimes I felt re-entry) into the world to the best of my ability, and what is more—and felt so wonderful—we began to love one another. ("Writing" 357)

Walker goes on to say that at first the characters came for short visits, and then they began to stay for longer and longer periods of time. Like Twain, once she returned to the book, she completed it in record time, much to her amazement and sadness—again like Twain—for she had grown to love and understand and identify with each of her characters. She undertook with them a journey of discovery, a journey whose conclusion is far from being known at the start of the project.

Twain, too, learned to be quiet—as quiet as a man like Twain could be—as he listened to the black and poor white voices from his childhood, voices he had almost forgotten. While Twain waited for his imaginative tank to refill, "everything was happening." Jim and Huck learned more about each other as well as about life and society away from the Mississippi. Much happened to Twain, and then he was ready with his enriched characters to resume the narrative as a personal, as well as sociohistorical, journey of discovery. Many of the causes and effects, as well as affects, of what Twain saw as cultural and racial inequality, religious hypocrisy, family disintegration, and a blind love affair with anything foreign occur in the novel's midsection.

A variety of incidents in the midsection of the novel make it crucial. The duke and the king are integral components of Huck's lesson in inhumanity and hypocrisy. In the encounters with the communities and families of slaves, including their masters, Twain stresses even more our need for understanding the antebellum dynamic. Seemingly paradoxical encounters round out Huck's education in humanity and inhumanity. We also witness how Jim makes meaning on several different levels. Twain methodically and persuasively reveals to us the "hidden and invisible" world of the slave along with the community's encoded language. Unlike other writers who could not resist adding authorial oversight, such as Frances Ellen Watkins Harper, for example, in *Iola Leroy*, Twain surrounds the reader with the community, as he does Huck. As the action and language unfold, Twain achieves the sense of immediacy and quandary that a white southerner like Huck would realistically experience.

By placing Jim and Huck in a context larger and less insulated than the raft and the river, Twain also allows the audience to witness the southern slave as a trickster figure rather than as the happy, ignorant darkey of the nineteenth-century stereotype.[4] When the situation demands such survival behavior, Twain offers a teasing glimpse of this face of slavery. He opens up not just the ultimate dialectic between Huck and Jim but a dialogue among the other characters, the peripheral characters, and, more importantly, a dialogue with the audience. If Huck and Jim had not passed Cairo, the last road to freedom for Jim, the novel would necessarily have ended without any real, profound truths, and few southern and northern myths would be discovered.

Passing Cairo gives Huck and Jim the opportunity to reexamine, and, consequently, reevaluate a range of Old South myths and reject them. Rather than giving us one more romanticized fiction about mistreated slaves and their indomitable but silent spirit, Twain dodges logic by letting his characters continue in the wrong direction, flinging us into the paradoxes of the mythic South.

The story of Jim *per se* is not unique. Hundreds of escape narratives reported flights of freedom in periodicals of the day as well as in published narratives and oral lectures. Of course, running toward freedom was no simple or easy matter. African American periodicals carried numerous stories both of slaves who attempted and failed to escape and of those who successfully found freedom. Even before the presumed time of the novel, *The Colored American* carried in its 7 July 1838 edition the following stories and speeches that focused on the runaway slave: "Speech of Mr. Gilette to the Legislature of Connecticut, May 1838," "$160.00 Reward," "Extract of a Letter from a gentleman in Georgia to his friend in Newark," and "Slavery." The perceived necessity for these accounts only increased. Note several of the sections in *Douglass' Monthly*, January 1859, twenty-one years later: "A Story of the Underground Railroad," "Convicted of Killing a Slave," "How the Case Stands," "History of the Amistad Case," "Women and Slavery," "The Peculiar Institution—A Man Sells his own Daughter," and "Old D.D.'s and Slavery." As these reports reveal, the straightest and most direct path to freedom was not always possible but was compounded with sexuality, miscegenation, and mortality. Success required self-reliance as well as reliance on others sympathetic to abolition, a treacherous journey that Twain entices the audience to witness through comedy and melodrama.

Chapter 16 begins with the now "voiced" and visible Jim expressing

his unabated anticipation of freedom, embodied in the crucial naviga-
tional site: Cairo. Without Cairo, Jim would "be in the slave country
again and no more show for freedom" (123). Up to this point, although
Huck seems to understand Jim, the man, he has not really contem-
plated the personal and social implications of his assuming the role of
abolitionist on Jim's behalf or of Jim's grasping the ephemeral dream
of freedom: "Well, I can tell you it made me all over trembly and fever-
ish, too, to hear him, because I begun to get it through my head that he
was most free—and who was to blame for it? Why, *me*. I couldn't
get that out of my conscience, no how nor no way. It got to troubling
me so I couldn't rest; I couldn't stay still in one place. It hadn't ever
come home to me before, what this thing was that I was doing. But
now it did; and it staid with me, and scorched me more and more" (123).

The physical and vocal juxtaposition Twain establishes here between Huck and Jim is critical in that Jim completely understands the
tenuousness of his position of slavery/freedom; Huck is beginning to
understand the extent of a commitment, a commitment that stands in
direct contradiction to what he has been taught, has observed, and has
believed. Huck at this point has trouble accepting such a commitment.
By placing the characters in such distinctive, contrastive positions,
Twain engages the audience in complementary psychological aspects
of the Jim dilemma. The reader identifies not with Jim alone or with
Huck but with each representative mental attitude simultaneously.
Whether we agree or disagree with Huck or Jim, Twain thrusts us into
their world. If we align ourselves with Huck's awakening, we question
many of our own social premises about property and authority.

For the African American reading audience, recognition and acknowledgment in this section is easy to achieve as it relates to Jim.
African Americans of free or slave ancestry identify with the ideal of

ultimate freedom, as their own contemporary and modern African American periodicals verify. A modern African American audience may find it more difficult, though, to identify with or understand Huck's plight. For the most part, we become impatient with his deliberations. Huck's subsequent personal logomachy with his conscience slows down the action, though. Important resonances with the earlier verbal battles have foreshadowed this outcome.

Huck's thinking shifts from the naively innocent racist point of view in the first third of the novel. The microcosmic voice of the slaveholding South becomes more prominent in his internal dialogue as he accepts an increasing degree of involvement in Jim's situation:

I tried to make out to myself that *I* warn't to blame, because *I* didn't run Jim off from his rightful owner; but it warn't no use, conscience up and says, every time, "But you knowed he was running for his freedom, and you could a paddled ashore and told somebody." . . . Conscience says to me, "What had poor Miss Watson done to you, that you could see her nigger go off right under your eyes and never say one single word? What did that poor old woman do to you, that you could treat her so mean? Why, she tried to learn you your book, she tried to learn you your manners, she tried to be good to you every way she knowed how. *That*'s what she done." (123)

Indeed, what a way to treat a poor, old woman who, though she traffics in human beings—buying, selling, and separating families—represents the emblem of Christian love and veracity with which Huck is all too familiar.

Twain through the art of his satire has made the ugly seem so palatable that the reader along with Huck momentarily forgets his position before revolting from it. Huck needs more time to assimilate all that is happening to him if his transformation is to be authentic, substantive, and complete. Such slow discovery seems a luxury with which the modern audience, particularly those who find the novel racist, is impatient. Opponents would have us believe that Huck's psychological and moral dilemma is simple avoidance. The text does not support that position, however. It should not be lightly dismissed that Huck wishes he were dead, for death would obviate the need to make the decision facing him between socially endorsed racism and ostracized humanity. A solution favoring either Jim or Miss Watson would require that he reject inculcated pretruths, or idols, or newly evolving truths. What Harriet Beecher Stowe had dramatized as a dialogue between the Shelbys in *Uncle Tom's Cabin* Twain now makes into interior monologue, both sensing the ambiguities of the national conscience.

It may seem that the last thing high school and college students want to know about is one more Renaissance or seventeenth-century philosopher, but understanding Francis Bacon's description, in *Novum Organum*, of how we as humans deal with ultimate truths can shed some light on the process that claims Huck. Bacon proposes that we begin with an idea or belief that, because of our environment, transforms to a filial, or familial, truth that progresses to a societal truth and finally to a universal truth. Once this belief evolves into a universal truth, it often becomes an idol. Bacon's ideas, radical for his time (as were Twain's), assert that because our idols are so comfortable and so familiar, we resist change; we resist discovering something very different from that which we hold true. If we risk examining our idols, we may discover our idols to be meaningless, a frightening prospect to human beings. Like Bacon, Twain is intensely aware of the power of conceptualization. It is for this reason that he forces Huck and the reader to reassess previously held truths, to fully understand them and their impact and to question whether the belief is as valid as originally thought. His goal is to provide the reader with a venue for refocusing and, if necessary, amending static truths. Huck's suicidal feeling reflects the intensity of the personal and moral conflict at the basis of this Baconian recognition.

Jim's continued verbalization of his dream heightens Huck's apprehension, particularly when Jim shatters the central myth that the slave family did not truly experience filial affection, responsibility, and duty. He reveals to Huck his plan first to purchase his wife, who is on another plantation, and then to work together with her to purchase their children. What chills—freezes—Huck's body and soul is Jim's implacable resolve to procure an "Ab'litionist to go and steal them" if the masters refuse to sell (124). This voice expands the voice on Jackson's Island into a voice of decisive action and strategy. The fascinating irony here lies with Huck Finn's "astonishment" and deduction that Jim has just developed these yearnings and this voice. Huck is actually speaking for post-Reconstruction readers who do not feel the same intensity over slavery that antebellum and Reconstruction social thinkers felt. In truth, Jim allows this outburst of rebellious sentiments here because he feels safe with Huck and because, perhaps for the first time in his life, freedom is within reach. Jim has always wanted his family back, whole, as Twain later reveals more clearly; only now does he express the idea to a white.

Twain's puns and oxymorons on the notion of stealing one's own children, slave children, is a source of agitation and distress for many African American readers. The idea that Huck feels embarrassed for Jim seems to them wholly unconscionable. However, in the context of Huck's world, even as it is deconstructing, such a sentiment is entirely within reason. Twain's rendering of the southern mindset shows us that Huck misses the nuances of stealing conjoined with slavery. Linguistic niceties are an object of ironic recasting in his voice. As Alexis de Tocqueville observed, most white southerners took it for granted that "[t]he Negro enters upon slavery as soon as he is born, nay, he may have been purchased in the womb, and have begun his slavery before he began his existence" (333). The difference is that de Tocqueville saw that the nation would pay a terrible price for slavery; Huck experiences such pre-vision only as his personal struggle.

In contrast to Huck, northern abolitionist counterparts viewed "stealing" as not only ethical and moral but legal as well, as documented in *Mirror of Liberty*, a nineteenth-century African American periodical, first published on 4 July 1838 with the motto "LIBERTY IS THE WORD FOR ME—ABOVE ALL, LIBERTY." Edited by activist David Ruggles, an African American, it was sustained by more than one ethnic community or economic class. Ruggles, a Connecticut native, was an activist in the New York Committee of Vigilance and like Harriet Tubman was maligned and "wanted" by every proslavery individual and group, as well as by some pseudoabolitionists.[5] How passionate individuals such as Ruggles could actualize their beliefs is clear in his account of the "Brooklyn Affair," in which Ruggles takes it upon himself to liberate, or "steal," a New York slave-woman, Charity ("*New York Gazette*" 2).

Unlike Ruggles, whose focus is always clear and implacable, Huck is in a state of uncertainty when he leaves the raft and goes to confirm Cairo. Jim sends Huck off with persuasive rhetoric that places Huck psychologically in an untenable and paradoxical position: "Pooty soon I'll be a-shout'n for joy, en I'll say, it's all on accounts o' Huck; I's a free man, en I couldn't ever ben free ef it hadn' ben for Huck; Huck done it. Jim won't ever forgit you, Huck; you's de bes' fren' Jim's ever had; en you's de *only* fren' ole Jim's got now. . . . Dah you goes, de ole true

Huck; de on'y white genlman dat ever kep' his promise to ole Jim" (124). There seems no doubt of his sincerity. Jim's genuine appreciation is frequently noted, but what is often disregarded is his even more fascinating logic. Here is another opportunity to observe Jim manipulating the language. As Fishkin has asserted in a lecture, "Twain imbued Jim with the linguistic ability to hear, process, and construct the appropriate message to the Southern hearer that would satisfy, or rather placate, him." At the same time, the slave would yet consciously maintain a subtextual meaning that only the slave and the slave community could translate. As readers, we feel this shifty undercurrent by virtue of two words, "white genlman," that forcibly remind us—and Huck as well—of the context surrounding the personal moment.

Jim is an African American man who, after some reticence on the island, decides to trust the white boy. This white boy has his own plan for escape and is not an abolitionist. No one has to tell Jim Huck's position on the slavery issue. A consistent diet of revelation and persuasion anchored in reassurance is necessary, for he knows they will encounter other influences along the journey to freedom. Masterfully, Jim succeeds in conveying his sincere love and gratitude to Huck, once again placing on Huck's heart and conscience, and on the reader's conscience, the import of the relationship they have thus far forged together. Huck is the friend, the only friend, the only white friend Jim has ever had. He is also the passport, the only one who can give Jim what he now needs, his access to freedom. Jim ensures that no matter whom Huck meets or what social circumstances he might encounter, he will feel his singularity as an actor outside of—and above—his real class allegiance as construed by the slaveholding society. When he meets the two bounty hunters, for example, Huck shows the result of this development. His trying to tell the "truth" about Jim's ethnicity fails, and he transforms Jim not only into a white man but into Pap-Jim Finn. Huck, responding subliminally to Jim's parting words, constructs an intricate lie on a lie. He "promises" the hunters, "I won't let no runaway niggers get by me if I can help it" (127).

What makes this section so interesting and compelling is that Jim is far from being invisible in it. He has been the silent observer, yes, but he has consciously elected to be silent only when the situation merited such action:

I went into the wigwam; Jim warn't there. I looked all around; he warn't anywhere. I says:

"Jim!"

"Here I is, Huck. Is dey out o' sight yit? Don't talk loud."

He was in the river . . . with just his nose out.

"I was a-listenin' to all de talk, en I slips into de river en was gwyne to shove for sho' if dey come aboard. Den I was gwyne to swim to de raf' agin when dey was gone. But lawsy, how you did fool 'em, Huck! Dat *wuz* de smartes' dodge! I tell you, chile, I' speck it save' ole Jim—ole Jim ain't gwyne to forgit you for dat, honey." (128)

If we argue here that Jim "loses" his voice and, thereby, any gain of place and visibility previously realized, then it seems that we would also have to find his actions and thought processes flawed. Commending Huck for his wit and loyalty could then be construed as an additional indication that Jim lacks substance.

However, Jim's actions and reactions in this scene are all very logical. They are both substantive and quite realistic for the time. His previous admonition to Huck and the commendation he pays Huck after the encounter with the two bounty hunters are master strokes. They reveal the adaptability of voice, the presence a southern slave had to have to survive, whether on the plantation or on the road to freedom. As we see here, Jim's is a presence that is and is not, as the situation dictates. When Huck's development requires, Jim speaks; he displays the intellectual acumen to know what is required. Even when it seems that he is not directly involved with an action, he continues to exert some control over it. The experience of running away was survived as much by this kind of wit and wisdom as it was by tenacity and brute strength. In fact, brute strength was the last criterion for embarking on the road toward freedom, as narratives like those of Henry "Box" Brown tell us.

As further indication that Jim's actions were representative, we have only to look once more to the periodicals and fiction. Consider, for example, an 1865 article in *The Freedman*, a monthly magazine "devoted to the interests of the four millions of freed people in the United States of America." The following was recounted by the Rev. Samuel Garratt, M.A.:

It is not so well known as it ought to be in this country how great the effort was with which while the war lasted negroes made their escape from slavery. An impression, which must be ascribed to a Divine influence, that the war would result in their deliverance, and that like the Israelites of old they had only to "stand still and see the salvation of the Lord," a favourite text with many of them, restrained them from acts of violence, and from attempting flight under hopeless circumstances.

But when escape was possible they underwent every risk and hardship to effect it. An eye-witness [Dr. Tomkins] relates how while a battle was raging in the neighborhood he saw numbers of men, women and children arrive within the Federal lines, who had taken that opportunity of slipping into freedom. "They had no shelter, little clothing, and no food. . . . They arrived in the evening, some of them having made a detour of sixty miles, footsore of course and wearied. . . . I took aside nearly fifty of them. 'Are you not tired,' said I, 'and do you not wish yourself back again at the old home?' 'Not so tired as we were last night,' said one of them, with hope beaming in his countenance; 'and though we should like to go back to the old place, we came here because we were resolved to be free.' " (1 October 1965, 1-2)

Harper's *Iola Leroy* and Hopkins's *Contending Forces*, along with a number of slave narratives, further reflect this mindset, the ironic paradox of "visibility and voice." One has only to refer to monographs like Philip Bruce's *The Plantation Negro as Freedman* as well as the southern periodicals of the day to understand that the way the South viewed itself—as a successful economic system and standard-bearer of genteel living—was only possible within the parameters of slavery. In the South this is yet a sensitive issue, for acknowledgment of it requires that such indignities did occur routinely.

As at the conclusion of the novel's first third and in Huck's scouting for Cairo at the beginning of the midsection, Jim once more affirms their relationship with subtlety and genuine emotion. Note his use of the plural, for he is now not thinking only of himself and his family but of Huck Finn, too: "We's safe, Huck, we's safe! Jump up and crack yo' heels, dat's de good ole Cairo at las', I jis knows it!" (124). Jim's rhetorical reaffirmation prepares Huck and the audience for more intricately woven encounters with the inhumanities of slavery and the general dis-ease and inhumanity of the mythic, noblesse oblige South. Huck's deliberation about stealing will be further amplified and explored as he and Jim travel farther south. Twain will demystify the real life of a slave, a runaway slave, staunch proslavery advocates, "benevolent" slave owners, ambivalent slave owners, unscrupulous bounty hunters, and confidence men. Twain renders all these creatures panoramically through the mind and perspective of an adolescent boy who must make up his southern mind about the issue in the South. He will reserve the demystification of Huck, Tom, and ourselves for the novel's ending.

Twain's is an interesting twist on a traditional trait of the Menippean satire, the symposium, and we have much to gain by seeing it in this perspective. Although symposium in the Platonic sense means a convivial coming together for talk and food, the Menippean symposium includes a variety of speakers and topics focused on "ideas and cultural interests." It merges an encyclopedic analysis of "intellectual themes and attitudes" with the symposium's rhetorical purpose (Frye 310-11). Rather than limited to one room, one central character, or one home, Twain's symposium is the journey and episodic encounters down the Mississippi. The convivial discussion is parodic burlesque and language manipulation. As with Chapter 16, successive chapters are often targeted by critics as being disappointing scenes in which, even when Jim is present, Twain allows Huck and others to relegate Jim to the role of caricature. They suggest that he takes this subservient role for no reason and see him as losing his previously gained importance. On the contrary, I think Jim loses no importance and is not caricatured but burlesqued with his conscious consent. Before delving into the burlesque scenes, however, let us look at how Twain reconstructs the idea and purpose of the symposium.

Twain constructs sixteen symposia-like scenes in which Huck must experience other views of slavery, freedom, responsibility, honesty, and family. Of the sixteen symposia, the most notable are Huck's reunion with Jim while at the Grangerfords (Chapter 18), Huck's description of slavery to Joanna Wilks (Chapter 26), the selling of the Wilks's slave family (Chapter 27), and the often-attacked conclusion of the novel, where Tom frees the manumitted slave (Chapters 34-43).

With the first three examples Twain places Huck in a situation where he must observe slavery as it is exposed around him. He must see its anomalies in the very people he naively considers upper-class—to him, therefore, necessarily intelligent, ethical, and trustworthy. He must listen to observations about slavery unfamiliar to not only to him but to the modern audience as well. Twain cleverly establishes some physical distance between Huck and Jim so that we can observe and listen to Huck's further (re)visioning of humanity. The separation enables us also to see how Jim survives by his wits. The separateness of Huck and Jim, then, is not only natural and realistic for the situation, for who would openly reconnoiter if not Huck, but stylistically and thematically important too. The novel maintains its cohesion and coherence with Twain's ultimate message. The audience is made acutely aware of the dis-ease of slavery. Only later might we see this also in the failure of Reconstruction.

Following Chapter 16, the next logical phase of the journey of empirical discovery and learning is to position Jim and Huck in a larger, less controlled environment where the variables are seemingly random. Chapters 17 and 18 provide one of the first uncontrolled, pragmatic learning intrusions for Huck, as well as for the audience. We see how a plantation functioned and how the slaves were perceived by slave-holding families. Twain juxtaposes this image against the ways slaves themselves survived in communities formed in spite of the master's dictates. Twain's artistic aim here is to open up to examination the slave-holding South's perception of itself—its aristocracy, pseudoaristocracy, middle class, and working class, as well as the social misfits represented earlier by Pap Finn and now by the drunken Boggs.

Chapter 16 concludes with Jim and Huck deducing that they have passed Cairo and with the climactic collision of the steamboat and the raft. Jim and Huck are separated. Jim's assessment of the catastrophe articulates a fear that was familiar to every runaway slave—failure: "Po' niggers can't have no luck. I awluz' 'spected dat rattle-snake skin warn't done wid its work" (129). Such a dire view was not uncommon among runaways or the general slave population. Accounts of failure and frustration passed from slave community to slave community, told by slaves themselves and slave owners who sought to control by creating an atmosphere of fear and subservience. In the story by "Uncle" Billy McCrae from Jasper, Texas, for example, we see the penalty for being caught or for simply failing in an escape plan: "We use' to go home and steal bread an' stuff and poke it through the little bars to the prisoners [caught runaways]. We was boys. That's right here in Jasper. An' it was an ol' log jail house. . . . An' I recollect one time, we was all looking at it. An' they brought in, had hounds. An' they brought them hound in and brought three nigger with them hound, runaway niggers, you know, caught in the wood. And they, right, across, right at the creek there, they take them niggers and put them on a log lay them down an' fasten them. An whip them. You hear them niggers hollering an' praying on them logs. An' there was a nigger bring them in. Then they take them out down there an' put them in jail" (qtd. in Bailey, Maylor, and Kukor-Avila 43-44). Mr. McCrae's experience generally parallels what Jim and Huck experience. There is the same sense of frustration and anxiety, yet in the midst of it the slave community acts, providing food and sustenance for the runaways. Jack and his community, we will soon learn, have hidden and fed Jim at the Grangerfords. Over and over again, the slave's imperturbable sense of self-reliance and resilience emerges. While Twain was not specifically familiar with Mr. McCrae's account, he was familiar with similar ones such as that of Frederick Douglass. In the face of other more violent stories, the modesty of the experience belies its importance.

Twain re-creates Mr. McCrae's story in a brief, slanting vision. After the steamboat collision, Huck calls to an unresponsive Jim. Hearing the dogs, Huck, too, checks his motions: "I knowed better than to move another peg" (131). Once cleared by the owners of the plantation, Huck is matter-of-factly informed that should anyone else be with him, they will be shot on the spot. Fear of "others" is all pervasive, even before race is considered.

Huck's introduction to the Grangerfords shows us the southern idea of quality; people like the Grangerfords represent authoritative truth and order in Huck's experience. Their house itself is emblematic for Huck, but for the reader it is a microcosm of the continuing delusion of the South—the historical myth versus the tawdry real:

It was a mighty nice family, and a mighty nice house, too. I hadn't seen no house out in the country before that was so nice and had so much style. . . . This table had a cover made out of beautiful oil-cloth, with a red and blue spread-eagle painted on it, and a painted border all around. It come all the way from Philadelphia . . . . There was some books too, piled up perfectly exact, on each corner of the table. One was a big family Bible, full of pictures. One was "Pilgrim's Progress," about a man that left his family it didn't say why. I read considerable in it now and then. The statements was interesting, but tough. Another was "Friendship's Offering," full of beautiful stuff and poetry; but I didn't read the poetry. Another was Henry Clay's Speeches, and another was Dr. Gunn's Family Medicine. . . . They had pictures hung on the walls—mainly Washingtons and Lafayettes, and battles, and Highland Marys, and one called "Signing the Declaration." (136-37)[6]

The audience clearly sees that gaudy gentility and tinseled hypocrisy, but to Huck it is wholly imperceptible. The family sees no contradiction in having in the same room *Henry Clay's Speeches* and a picture of the signing of the Declaration of Independence. The contradiction embodies the theme Twain presents throughout the novel in various forms. Henry Clay, a slave owner, was a cofounder of the American Colonization Society, represented this country as senator, and drafted the Compromise of 1850, which strengthened the Fugitive Slave Act.[7] Having his speeches next to a representation of the signing of a document founded on freedom of the individual, independence, and mutual respect for difference symbolizes the pivotal irony on which the novel turns.

Of further interest, too, is that Huck is alone. For the psychological evolution that is taking place, he must confront each of his own learned truths, one at a time. Although having disappeared in person, Jim is present in Huck's mind. At this point, Huck must relate two formative but conflicting concepts: his emerging connection to Jim and the codes of behavior learned from Miss Watson and the widow. Here in the Grangerford library, Huck "understands" what composes the good, aristocratic Christian's library. The pictures in it all delineate love, freedom, independence, equality—the right to be an individual— symbols of freedom displayed in a home that denies freedom. Slaves serve behind Huck at the dining table; each person has his own special slave. Twain ensconces his character in the most conventional slavery setting just as he comes to question it. Huck, like Jim, observes, but is careful to blend invisibly into this world.

Chapter 18 continues the extended metaphor of southern noblesse oblige with the description of Col. Saul Grangerford. Huck is awed by him. Wilson Jeremiah Moses attributes this kind of captivation to an acquiescence by other classes, particularly "serfs and peasants," to the apparent superiority of the aristocracy and the bourgeoisie. Moses argues that without this acquiescence "the upper classes would have been deprived of their ostentatious, oppressive power" (158-59).[8] Twain would explicitly concur with this assessment in *A Connecticut Yankee in King Arthur's Court* in 1889. Note the simple declarative sentence of our young narrator: "Grangerford was a gentleman, you see" (143). Note, too, Huck's deliberate, rhetorical reiteration: "He was a gentleman all over; and so was his family" (143). "Blood will tell," and so Huck Finn deduces that Col. Grangerford's blood tells a tale of august presence and southern refinement: "He was well born, as the saying is, and that's worth as much in a man as it is in a horse, so the Widow Douglas said, and nobody ever denied that she was of the first aristocracy in our town; and pap he always said it, too, though he warn't no more quality than a mud-cat, himself" (143).[9] After such an assessment and characterization for himself and the audience, the scene continues to unfold when Huck is assigned his own personal slave, Jack: "Each person had their own nigger to wait on them—Buck, too. My nigger had a monstrous easy time, because I warn't used to having anybody do anything for me, but Buck's was on the jump most of the time" (144-45). Huck later tells us that Grangerford owned over a hundred slaves and several farms.

As Huck observes more about plantation life, he also learns about how the aristocracy handles its social "disagreements," for the Grangerfords are having a blood feud with the Shepherdsons. For Huck an internal comparison/contrast now begins without his ever being wholly conscious of it. Such approved and upstanding families as these are balanced against his relationship with Pap Finn and against his newly developing familial bonds with Jim. He encounters exquisite paradoxes like church-going with guns-at-the-ready. Southern life is fully juxtaposed with the "Romeo-and-Juliet" love affair of Sophia Grangerford and Harney Shepherdson. Love and death are easily interchangeable; there is no peace even through marriage. Huck shows us a world of moral chaos with only the smallest of comic demurs: "a hog is different" (149).

One of the recurring controversies for modern Twain readers is over Huck's behavior on the plantation. Huck easily adapts to the situation; he reassumes superiority over the southern African American slave. In other words, if Twain is not a closet racist, opponents assert, why does Huck simply accept the lifestyle at the Grangerfords, a style that includes every person having a dedicated slave? I think the explanation lies in the way Twain has so far revealed Huck's unique ability to question a given situation in spite of his own preconceptions. His questions to Buck about the feud and the reasons for its origin reconfirm Huck's continuing growth, particularly with relation to the issue of slavery and Jim. This world is insanely committed to perpetuating the violence implicit in its own history.

To complicate the situation even more, Huck soon realizes that "his assigned nigger" is not as ignorant, servile, silent, or invisible as we and he initially thought. When this slave comes to "Mars Jawge" (Huck in disguise) and asks him to follow so that he can show Huck "a whole stack o' water-moccasins," Huck follows, even though he thinks it a strange request (150). Twain thus gives us another example of the slave's masterful use of language to survive in a milieu where such mastery was lawfully forbidden. With the mask of the double voice in place, Jim and now Jack initiate Huck into the most vital of slave realities: all is not as it may appear. Huck follows Jack but really does not know why: "Thinks I, that's mighty curious; he said that yesterday. He oughter know a body don't love water-moccasins enough to go around hunting for them. What is he up to anyway?" (150). Twain as consummate realist, however overt he may seem elsewhere, disappears as completely as does any sign of outward rebellion in the plantation slaves.

What Huck finds, of course, is Jim, safely hidden away from danger and yet close enough to observe the Grangerfords and Huck. Contrary to the criticism that Jim disappears, yet again, because Twain did not know what to do with him, Jim's apparent invisibility and loss of voice are more productive and powerful than had he risked a meaningless capture and certain exposure. Has he been idle? Was he possibly waiting for Huck?

I waked him up, and I reckoned it was going to be a grand surprise to him to see me again, but it warn't. . . . Said he swum along behind me, that night, and heard me yell every time, but dasn't answer, because he didn't want nobody to pick *him* up, and take him into slavery again. Says he—

"I got hurt a little, en couldn't swim fas', so I wuz a considable ways behine you, towards de las'; when you landed I reck'ned I could ketch up wid you on de lan' 'doub havin' to shout at you, but when I see dat house I begin to go slow. I 'uz off too fur to hear what dey say to you—I wuz 'fraid o' de dogs—but when it 'uz all quiet agin, I knowed you's in de house, so I struck out for de woods to wait for day. Early in de mawnin' some er de niggers come along, gwyne to de fields, en dey tuck me en showed me dis place, whah de dogs can't track me on accounts o' de water, en dey brings me truck to eat every night, en tells me how you's a gitt'n along."

"Why didn't you tell my Jack to fetch me here sooner, Jim?"

"Well, 'twarn't no use to 'sturb you, Huck, tell we could do sumfn—but we's all right, now. I ben a-buyin' pots en pans en vittles, as I got a chanst, en a-patchin' up de raf', nights." (150-51)

So Jim, with the assistance of the slave community, has been busy observing, orchestrating, and rebuilding their means of escape. Jim reiterates his focus; Twain thus demonstrates his tenacity for the freedom quest even if he is not directly working with Huck Finn as his passport. While Huck has been involved with the feud, Jim, a slave sustained by the Grangerfords' slaves, has been busy preparing for their mutual escape.

As the time grows near and Jim is ready to depart, his link to the outside for knowing what is happening is the slave community's network. Jack, Huck's personal slave, brings Jim news of Huck's fate. Ironically, the initial report of Huck's "death" to Jim from Jack is incorrect but logically deduced. Jim, not wanting to believe the report but also unwilling to lose his opportunity, waits longer—but not too long: "I's jes' dis minute a startin' de raf' down towards de mouf er de crick, so's to be all ready for to shove out en leave soon as Jack comes agin en tells me for certain you *is* dead" (155). Just as on Jackson Island, Jim is consciously and deliberately in running mode, with or without Huck. But now he wants to go with him and risks his life for certainty. In the face of violent melodrama, the quiet heroism at the periphery is all but invisible. As Jim the character, so Twain the novelist: deadpan to the chapter's end, yet true to his purpose.

*   *   *

Jim's voice—Jim's choice—not Huck's, or Jack's has been dictating Jim's responses. For a while at least, on the river, which represents for Huck and Jim a center of quietness, both can feel free and easy. This raft is a center of control, of community, and of sanity. To Jim it is a place conducive for (re)memory, as Toni Morrison describes it, and free imagination—imagining for the first time in his "free" life how real freedom and a real, united family might feel. For Huck the river is a living, learning place where he can engage Jim in conversation or simply listen to him as a human being for the first time in his life. The journey on the raft has led Huck to understand Jim and his "kind" as something different—different from previous conceptions that made them less than human. Some of the most finely realized lyric moments in American literature are the immediate result in Chapter 19.

Although both characters become transformed on the river, the river is not, as T. S. Eliot asserts, the sole symbol making this novel a great novel. If the reader focuses exclusively on the image of the river as the primary controlling device of the narrative, then what the characters do, how they react, where they go, and even their eventual decisions are of little consequence. On this point, most of the novel's critics agree; the characters themselves form the nucleus of the novel, and the river, though it does provide the protean form for the narrative, is far from being the entity that, according to Eliot, "controls the voyage of Huck and Jim; that will not let them land in Cairo.... It is the River that separates and deposits Huck for a time in the Grangerford household; the River that re-unites them, and then compels upon them the unwelcomed company of the king and the duke" (vi). Eliot concludes that it is the River, therefore, that makes the book great. But it is not, finally. Its greatness comes from the fact that Huck and Jim now both have the possibility of full involvement in their humanity to-gether. We as readers realize this potential in the river's context, but the issue remains race.

The river provides an imaginative and geographic frame in which the narrative emerges. An ambiguous symbol, it offers a variety of pos-sibilities for either freedom or enslavement, depending on where the pair stop. As facilitator, the river is a source of tumultuous upheaval, but it also provides the "quiet" center in which Huck can reach en-lightenment and Jim can reveal himself. We know such changes are occurring, for example, when the tone and structure of the verbal bat-tles shift in the discussion on the origin of the stars in Chapter 19. Huck and Jim no longer battle for control over who will win the argu-ment. Huck listens to Jim's idea of how the stars came into being. And he surmises that Jim's idea that the moon births the stars is a reason-able one: nature, wonder, and mutuality now define their actions. The moment reveals them in a moment of spiritual beauty transcending race, just as it provides a natural metaphor for the condition.

Again, some twentieth-century readers, racially sensitive to what-ever Jim says, are irritated in an already agitated spot. They object to the fact that his notion of the origin of the stars involves superstition and African American folklore. We must stop to consider the impor-tance that folklore, myth, and superstition held in the nineteenth-century in all cultures. The nineteenth-century South was no exception, with its own share of lore, myth, and superstitions, some of which live on as grandmotherly nuggets of warnings, remedies, or homespun beliefs and some of which perpetuate racial separation and suspicion and fear.[10] Yet, critic David L. Smith has pointed out that superstition is one more significant tool of the slave for survival: "In assessing Jim's character, we should keep in mind that forethought, creativity, and shrewdness are qualities that racial discourse . . . denies to the Negro. In that sense, Jim's darkey performance . . . subverts the fundamental definition of darkey. For the Negro is defined to be an object, not a subject. But does an object construct a narrative? Viewed in this way, the fact of superstition, which traditionally connotes ignorance and unsophistication, becomes far less important than the ends to which superstition is put" (109-10).

Jim's articulation of lore and legend resembles that of the griot of old whose task it was to assure the continuance and health of the community and culture through song and story telling, or story making. Slave narratives, documents, and fictions reveal that wherever slaves found themselves, they continued spreading their wisdom and beliefs in spite of disruption, thereby maintaining some semblance of community. In these kinds of scenes throughout the novel, Twain isolates Huck and Jim. By doing so he shows that only a completely alternate world is possible, and he denies the fallacy of benevolent slavery. Interestingly, William Faulkner and Toni Morrison later revisit this theme, specifically in works such as Faulkner's *The Unvanquished, The Town, As I Lay Dying*, and Morrison's *Beloved*.

Twain elaborates on this alternate unity when Huck finds himself in another more complicated situation without Jim's physical presence but certainly with his psychological influence. The amplified episodes involving the duke and the king, Sherburn and Boggs, and later the Wilks sisters provide a gauge by which the audience can measure Huck's psychological progress toward (re)visioning a new truth.

Jim's adaptive transformation continues with the introduction of the duke and king. As we have seen, the runaway had to be inventive and quick-witted if freedom were to be attained. Numerous accounts chronicle the quick-wittedness of the runaway: Henry "Box" Brown, who shipped himself to Philadelphia in a box marked "This Side Up"; Uncle Sandy, who severed four fingers on his right hand in front of the slave catchers to make himself not only useless but not worth the killing; the Crafts, who posed not as the husband and wife they were but as servant and mistress to gain safe passage during the day on trains. As a late twentieth-century audience it is easy for us to say that Jim and Huck should have just said no to these obvious rogues. "Get off of our raft; you have no place here." But in their time, one question was forever on the mind of not only the runaway but also those who would help: Whom do I trust? Charles H. Nilon, in "Freeing the Free Negro," notes that serious dangers threatened both Jim and Huck: "Both river shores were dangerous: although Illinois was technically a free state, fugitive slave laws were in effect, and Huck too would have been subject to arrest" (66).

Numerous posted bills in the North warned escapees not to trust anyone, and many abolitionist periodicals warned runaways to be ever vigilant. Even those who were free had to be wary. Of the many examples, two are particularly interesting and valuable for helping the diverse audience of the twentieth century understand the hostile nineteenth-century environment. The first is excerpted from *Mirror of Liberty* and the second from Harper's *Iola Leroy*, Chapter 26, "Open Questions."

In the article "*New-York Gazette* and the Brooklyn Affair," David Ruggles recounts his struggles in attempting to free the slaves Charity, Jim, and Jesse, brought north by their masters, and to secure for them rightfully earned wages, which they have been denied despite the mistress's claims that these were indeed free people. Charity provides insight into the idea of trust. When confronted by Ruggles, the mistress counters, "They are *my* slaves, and they cannot receive wages" (italics mine). Ruggles counters with, "I thought you brought them here where they could be free, Mrs. Dodge." The verbal battle continues:

"Jim, Charity, and Jesse, are free as any body. Aint you!"

"Ah!" said the old woman, "I do not know that, mistress. I hear when the master come, he send us back."

"That is a mistake, aint it, Charity?"

"I don't know, I hear so, missee."

"Hav'nt I told you that you are free?"

"You told me to say so if any bode ask me, but you beat me here as much as ever, missee."

[Ruggles interjects here] "Why, If Mrs. Dodge brought you here to be free, she would not treat you ill but, on the contrary, she would be kind to you, and pay you wages."

"Wages!" says Charity.

"Oh no," says Mrs. D. "But I take good care of you."

"I have lived here four years, and never received a dollar, and this home-spun frock and linsey woolsey petticoats that I stand in, is my best dress."

"Come, I won't have so much talk, Charity. I suppose you have been after this person, to take you away."

Ruggles is successful in freeing Charity, but Jim and Jesse are returned into slavery.

A second example from Harper's *Iola Leroy*, Chapter 26, "Open Questions," includes Dr. Frank Latimer, an educated ex-slave, freed with his mother through Emancipation; slave runaway Robert Johnson; and the Reverend Carmicle. Carmicle is clearly colored, while Latimer and Johnson are light enough to "pass" as white. Attending a physician's conference, the three meet southern slavery sympathizer, Dr. Latrobe, who does not discern Frank Latimer's ethnicity: "We

Southerners will never submit to negro supremacy. We will never abandon our Caucasian civilization to an inferior race. . . . He is ignorant, poor, and clannish, and they may impact him as their policy would direct" (221). To this Latimer replies, "If the negro is ignorant, poor, and clannish, let us remember that in part of our land it was once a crime to teach him to read. If he is poor, for ages he was forced to bend to unrequited toil. If he is clannish, society has segregated him to himself" (222). This verbal contest continues until Carmicle and Johnson leave, and Latrobe summarizes the exchange to Latimer:

"There are niggers who are as white as I am, but the taint of blood is there and we always exclude it."

"How do you know it is there?" asked Dr. Gresham [another white physician in the company].

"Oh there are tricks of blood which always betray them. My eyes are more practiced than yours. I can always tell them. Now, that Johnson is as white as any man; but I knew he was a nigger the moment I saw him. I saw it in his eye." (229)

It is not until after Latrobe has heard Latimer's paper and declared both it and Latimer unqualified successes that Latimer reveals his real identity, shattering a southern stereotype:

"I hope," answered Dr. Latrobe, "that if you go South you will only sustain business relations with the negroes, and not commit the folly of equalizing yourself with them."

"Why not?" asked Dr. Latimer, steadily looking him in the eye.

"Because in equalizing yourself with them you drag us down; and our social customs must be kept intact."

"You have been associating with me at the convention for several days; I do not see that the contact has dragged you down, has it?"

"You! What has that got to do with associating with niggers?" asked Dr. Latrobe, curtly.

"The blood of that race is coursing through my veins. I am one of them," replied Dr. Latimer, proudly raising his head." (238)

Latrobe leaves, angered because he has been "deceived." Thus an African American author recognizes the ambiguity of detecting and assigning racial and social values by appearance. Twain in *Pudd'nhead Wilson* took up the same problem. For the slave seeking freedom and justice, the implicit threat lay everywhere, dependent on the self-interest on others.

It is in this environment that the duke and king enter the scene and are able to fool Huck, and initially Jim as well. Jim instinctively masks his real voice and assumes the voice of the slave once more, which, as we have seen, is a logical response. By the chapter's conclusion, Jim expresses what these men are and explores Huck's feelings about them as well:

When Jim called me to take the watch at four in the morning, he says—

"Huck, does you reck'n we gwyne to run acrost any mo' kings on dis trip?"

"No," I says, "I reckon not."

"Well," says he, "dat's all right, den. I doan' mine one er two kings, but dat's enough. Dis one's powerful drunk, en de duke ain' much better."

I found Jim had been trying to get him to talk French, so he could hear what it was like; but he said he had been in this country so long, and had so much trouble, he'd forgot it. (176)

Jim knows the score—the king and duke are not what they pretend to be. In his own way he puts them to the test, hence the inquiry into speaking French. In spite of the impending anxiety the situation provokes, we see Jim's in understanding that, imposters though they are, the duke and king are nevertheless in a position to compromise the two runaways. He wants no more kings or dukes to board the raft, but he will tolerate these. With this scene Twain continues the novel's thematic continuity and focus on characterization, reminding us, as earlier, to think of what defines a man.

Seemingly less logical is the way Jim identifies with the duke's plight. When the duke recounts being torn away from his family, "despised by the cold world, ragged, worn, heart-broken, and degraded," Jim the slave responds with recognition and empathy (163).[11] Jim's tolerance of the duke and dauphin is often viewed as impotence or Uncle Tomism, but it can also be interpreted as a strength. We have seen that the slave's ability to transcend his or her own despair and acknowledge another person in need, even a white southerner, was not atypical. Is such a response a sign of weakness and stupidity, or is it evidence of real understanding of what suffering means? More to the point, is it evidence of the slave's ability to transcend wrongs done to him in order to alleviate suffering in others? Jim's demeanor toward the duke and king, the recognition that allows anyone simply to exist, sharply contrasts Tom's desiring empty recognition for heroism.

Earlier, in Chapter 19, a slave is said to have alerted one of the scoundrels that the town intended to tar and feather him. Note the juxtaposition Twain constructs in this scene. The soon-to-be king sees only a "nigger [who] rousted me out this mornin', and told me the people was getherin' on the quiet, with their dogs and horses" (161). Yet the slave had acted out of his own experience, averting impending cruelty and suffering.

Twain's satiric irony here, of course, is that the duke and king are frauds, and Huck and Jim still accept them. The ultimate irony is that the duke, to achieve acknowledgment and voice, must weave an elaborate, completely false tale to persuade his victims. On the basis of his white race alone, they accept his made-up story. Jim, on the other hand, has to construct and constantly reiterate his real life story and position throughout the novel for Huck and for us. African American readers readily recognize this discrepancy between believability and trustworthiness, but they may too easily miss its importance by focusing on the frauds as frauds.[12]

Huck and Jim soon deduce that the scoundrels are not what they appear. The rascals further reveal their true natures when, like the bounty hunters, they inquire whether Huck has seen any runaways, coming uncomfortably close to uncovering the secret of Jim. As before, in order to protect Jim, Huck creates a tale to satisfy their curiosity. Huck relies on the traditional notion of slaves as negotiable and legal tender to be moved about at the pleasure and necessity of the present owner. The duke and king readily believe Huck's tale, a portrait that suggests the commonness of this practice, but gives us as readers one more reason to reject the milieu which was so commonplace as to serve as a blind.

Critics have contended that in this section Jim disappears or becomes docile once more. Upon closer examination, we see that Huck and Jim are actually working in tandem. When the time comes, for example, to go to the next town to "fix that thing"—that thing being Jim and the need to run the raft during the day—Jim wisely sends Huck: "We was out of coffee, so Jim said I better go along with them in the canoe and get some" (171). Not only are they getting supplies: more importantly, Huck and Jim maintain a close watch on the two untrustworthy "royals" at *Jim's* direction. One significant result of this expedition for Jim was a printed slave bill, designed by the king. He lies that this slave bill advertising Jim as a runaway is for the good of them all because now they can travel during the day and mask Jim as a runaway.

Needless to say, this scene is another source of anxiety for some African American students and parents because of the very notion of re-placing Jim into slavery. The bill itself and the wording, along with the emblematic image of the runaway slave, are the material of the horror of slavery itself. The king's design is, however, accurate for the period, according to reprints of such announcements in the periodicals. In fact, many of the abolitionist periodicals and magazines, both African American and white, devoted space to reprinting runaway slave bills to further solidify their antislavery position and expose an unfavorable view of the South to others. *Douglass' Monthly* does so with particular style and rhetorical fervor. With consciously employed rhetorical irony, Douglass, the former slave, called these feature items "Southern Gems," "A Few Southern Gems," and "Our Neighbors" and compelled his audience to identify with what they might not otherwise seek to know themselves:

NOTICE—$200. REWARD.

—My Negro man Miles about 35 or 40 years old, bright copper color, 5 feet 10 or 11 inches high, heavy made, and round face, runaway from my house in Marion county, KY., about 5 miles east of Lebanon, on the night of the 15th inst. Said boy has a wife at James Gastin's, Bedfordsville, Marion county. I have some fears said boy is making his way to a free State. He is very sensible and smart, and may have free papers. The said boy was well clothed with brown jean pants, and blue mixed coat, had also a black mixed boy $25 if taken in this county, if taken out of the county and in this State $100, out of the State $200, and secured in some jail so that I can get him.

William W. Mays.

Marion county, Nov. 16, 1858.

[from the *New Orleans Picayune*]
Fifty Dollars Reward.

RAN AWAY from the subscriber, on the night of the 16th inst., the black woman Sarah, aged about thirty-four years, born in the city, speaks French and English. She has a scar on her right temple, and has lost most of her upper front teeth; has a sharp face, and is usually dressed in mourning; will likely be found in the School District. The above reward will be paid on her apprehension and delivery to A. Thompson, 13th St. Ferdinand street, Third District.

RUNAWAY NEGRO—Committed to the jail of Upshur Co. On the 26th of July, a runaway negro boy, who says his name is John, and that he belongs to Phil Thompson, who resides in the city of Houston, Harris Co., Texas. The said boy is about 25 years of age, rather slender built, about 5 feet 7 or 8 inches high, rather copper colored, and says he is a blacksmith by trade.

The owner is requested to come forward, prove property, pay charges and take him away, or he will be dealt with according to law.

J. H. Trowell, Dep. Sheriff, U.C.

Gilmer, Texas, Aug.2, '58.

These notices bear the same graphics as the king's bill of notice.

Why include such a thing as a slave bill in a literary work that is supposed to be against slavery? Like Douglass, Twain accomplishes through his description of such a bill an active engagement with his readers, compelling us to understand, some for the first time, the essence of an actual slave bill. Readers who have bonded with Jim also comprehend how it makes him feel, sensations that will be brought back late in the novel in Tom Sawyer's heraldic rendering. The scene also shows how easy it was to brand *any* African American a runaway. No hint of doubt about the viability or the ethics of such a scheme ever crosses our character's minds, including Jim's. Of course the duke and king's scheme will work. Pap Finn has already prepared the audience for such a possibility when he wondered why the professor was not being auctioned. Twain has created audience recognition and acknowledgment. We gain a painful but thought-provoking image: "The reading [of the mock slave bill] was all about Jim, and just described him to a dot. It said he run away from St. Jacques' plantation, forty mile below New Orleans, last winter, and likely went north, and whoever would catch him and send him back, he could have the reward and expenses" (176). Twain further enhances, or amplifies, this scene by allowing the king and duke to act in their true natures. Naturally suspicious, they recommend tying Jim up during the day. The duke says, "Whenever we see anybody coming, we can tie Jim hand and foot with a rope, and lay him in the wigwam and show this handbill and say we captured him up the river, and were too poor to travel on a steamboat, so we got this little raft on credit from our friends and are going down to get the reward. Handcuffs and chains would look still better on Jim, but it wouldn't go well with the story of us being so poor. Too much like jewelery. Ropes are the correct thing—we must preserve the unities, as we say on the boards" (176).

The elaborate satirical discussion on just how to restrain Jim reveals the seriousness and the earnestness of the king's and duke's lack of respect and simple humanity toward Jim. Although a painful spectacle, it foreshadows Chapter 31 and contrasts Huck's concern for Jim with the way the king and duke perceive him as other, or as David Smith remarks, "object" (110). Although Huck and Jim can identify and empathize, initially, with the sufferings and injustices done to the king and duke, the reverse is not true. The two "royals" embody the frequent sentiment of those in the (un)reconstructed South that no one suffered as they had been made to suffer. The duke succinctly articulates this view when he has been bested by the king in a struggle over who will sleep in which bed: " 'Tis my fate to be always ground into the mire under the iron heel of oppression. Misfortune has broken my once haughty spirit; I yield, I submit; 'tis my fate. I am alone in the world—let me suffer; I can bear it" (168). When we juxtapose this over-acted scene with the true adversities of not only the slaves thus far encountered but the dangers surrounding all African Americans in the book, such as the professor from the North, we see satire at its most acute. These sleazy hustlers, of course, do not know what real spiritual suffering means: to yield self and dignity to fellow humans who view you as nothing more than chattel.

The succeeding episodes allow Huck to encounter other, apparently peripheral southern African Americans. When Huck witnesses Sherburn's cold-blooded killing of "the best-naturedest old fool in Arkansaw," Boggs (184), he also witnesses something of equal importance—the attempted lynching of Sherburn and the reaction to this impending action by the southern slaves. Chapter 22 begins with Huck's describing the slaves and the growing lynch mob: "They swarmed up the street towards Sherburn's house, a-whooping and yelling and raging like Injuns, and everything had to clear the way or get run over and tromped to mush, and it was awful to see. Children was heeling it ahead of the mob, screaming and trying to get out of the way; and every window along the road was full of women's heads, and there was nigger boys in every tree, and bucks and wenches looking over every fence; and as soon as the mob would get nearly to them they would break and skaddle back out of reach" (189). The white children are actually on the ground with the mob, albeit simultaneously excited and terrified; the African American slaves are ever-watchful but at a safe and fearful distance. The slaves are in trees, behind fences—out of sight completely—as the mob rages. Huck witnesses and faithfully reports.

This scene, just as it is rendered, exacerbates already tense recognition problems with African American readers because of Huck's use of more denigrating and stereotyping words: *bucks, wenches,* and, of course, *nigger boys.* The primary question would obviously be, could Twain have used other, less offensive words and still accomplished his persuasive purpose? The term *wench,* for example, was a common southern reference for African American women slaves of breeding age, according to reference works of the time (*Webster's Dictionary,* 1828-32, and *Bartlett's,* 1848). Compare Twain's rendering above with that of John Wallace, a Twain opponent who decided to expurgate what he considered racially offensive words and phrases from the novel for the sake and self-esteem of students, particularly African American students: "Children was heeling it ahead of the mob, screaming and trying to get out of the way; and every window along the road was full of women's heads, and there was boys in every tree, and bucks and wenches looking over every fence; and as soon as the mob would get nearly to them they would break and skaddle back out of reach" (Wallace 110-11). Wallace blurs the frenzied psyche of a lynch mob and blurs the distinction of race, including the vital trait of survival refined and mastered by the slaves. Wallace's deliberate graying of the racist terms *buck* and *wench* by deleting from the series "nig-ger boys" compromises the distinctive dual image Huck witnesses. Twain is depicting a vision, which if we see it, adds further meaning to our dilemma with Jim. The slaves, unlike the whites, cannot come to the fore to observe the mob solely for the taste of spectacle. They ob-serve, as they must, to know what is developing around them. That they and only they in Twain's version "break and skaddle back out of reach" with alacrity as the mob approaches them shows their aware-ness of the immediate danger. The tenacity and blood lust of the mob creates an indisputable difference between the two groups. We see this scene in full color, color articulated in southern terms. Erasing the race factor diminishes and cheapens the role of blacks in the novel. Whites have no reason to run from this lynch mob. Wallace's expur-gated scene fails to depict this difference, the need for special survival skills and acumen of the African American slave.

The subsequent action provides a corollary to the psychology of the lynch mob. Twain uses Sherburn to describe not just this specific lynch but also to provide substantial commentary on the existence and purpose of the southern lynch mob, which existed primarily to hang and to maim, physically and psychologically, African Americans. Lerone Bennett, Jr., in *Before the Mayflower: A History of Black America*, describes the reality of southern mobs: "The plan: reduce blacks to po-litical impotence. How? By the boldest and most ruthless political op-eration in American history. By stealth and murder, by economic intimidation and political assassinations, by the use of political terror, by the braining of the baby in its mother's arms, the slaying of the husband at his wife's feet, the raping of the wife before the husband's eyes. By fear. Soon the South was honeycombed with secret organiza-tions: the Knights of the White Camellia, the Red Shirts, the White

League, Mother's Little Helpers and the Baseball Club of the First Baptist Church" and, of course, the Ku Klux Klan, originally formed in 1867 as a reaction to the freeing of blacks (231).

Characteristic of such groups was that they usually made their masked appearances at night, as Colonel Sherburn notes:

"The idea of *you* lynching anybody! It's amusing. The idea of you thinking you had pluck enough to lynch a *man*! Because you're brave enough to tar and feather poor friendless cast-out women that come along here, did that make you think you had grit enough to lay your hands on a *man*? Why, a *man's* safe in the hands of ten thousand of your kind—as long as it's day-time and you're not behind him. . . .

"The average man's a coward. In the North he lets anybody walk over him that wants to, and goes home and prays for a humble spirit to bear it. In the South one man, all by himself, has stopped a full stage of men, in the day-time, and robbed the lot. . . . Why don't your juries hang murderers? Because they're afraid the man's friends will shoot them in the back, in the dark—and it's just what they *would* do.

"So they always acquit; and then a *man* goes in the night, with a hundred masked cowards at his back, and lynches the rascal. Your mistake is, that you didn't bring a man with you; that's one mistake, and the other is that you didn't come in the dark, and fetch your masks. . . .

"The pitifulest thing out is a mob; that's what an army is—a mob; they don't fight with courage that's born in them, but with courage that's borrowed from their mass, and from their officers. . . . If any real lynching's going to be done, it will be done in the dark, Southern fashion; and when they come they'll bring their masks, and fetch a *man* along. Now *leave*—and take your half-a-man with you." (190-91)

In the dark, "Southern fashion," and in complete anonymity, the lynch mob was not only a tangible threat for the powerless but a frightening one that makes another transformative impression on Huck Finn. For the reader to see with any depth the contrast between the whites' reactions to the mob and those of the African Americans, Twain's clear distinction between the two groups in Huck's description is essential. Only with that racial distinction, however distasteful it may seem, can Huck and the audience identify the disturbing and loathsome essence of the southern lynch mob. Only later will he throw Jim into a lynch mob's hands. Had he done so thus early in the novel, grim realism might have replaced satire, ending Jim's part in the action all together.

Juxtaposed to the depiction of lynching is Huck's revelatory personal insight, in Chapter 23, that Jim cared just as much for his people as white people do for theirs. Huck hears Jim moaning and mourning to himself, when Jim thinks Huck is asleep. The reader remembers those early verbal battles between Jim and Huck about family, harems, boarding houses, and wisdom. Although they may have seemed humorous but perhaps not vital to plot development, those discussions and others in the novel's first third have prepared the reader for what transpires here. Huck, a product of his environment, could not initially identify Jim as a loving, caring husband and father. But now, in a major turning point in the novel, he sees a father who is most contrite for his mistakes.

Twain elevates Jim to a stature in this chapter unparalleled by any characters yet introduced. Notably, he does so just after Colonel Sherburn's extended definition on what makes a man. In one crystalline moment, Jim's manhood emerges. Here is a man who has undertaken the most dangerous quest possible for a southern African American in the nineteenth century. Here is a man who can show emotion over the loss of his family. Here is a man who shares with his friend a dark truth about himself as a father:

"What makes me feel so bad dis time, 'uz bekase I hear sumpn over yonder on de bank like a whack, er a slam, while ago, en it mine me er de time I treat my little 'Lizabeth so ornery. She warn't on'y 'bout fo' year ole, en she tuck de sk'yarlet-fever, en had a powful rough spell; but she got well, en one day she was a-stannin' aroun', en I says to her, I says:

"   'Shet de do'.'

"She never done it; jis' stood dah, kiner smilin' up at me. It make me mad; en I says agin, mighty loud, I says:

"   'Doan' you hear me?—shet de do'!'

"She jis' stood de same way, kiner smilin' up. I was a-bilin'! I says:

"   'I lay I *make* you mine!'

"En wid dat I fetch' her a slap side de head dat sont her a-sprawlin'. Den I went into de yuther room, en 'uz gone 'bout ten minutes; en when I come back, dah was dat do' a-stannin' open *yit*, en dat chile stannin' mos' right in it, a-lookin' down and mournin', en de tears runnin' down. My, but I *wuz* mad, I was agwyne for de chile, but jis' den—it was a do' dat open innerds—jis' den, 'long come de wind en slam it to, behine de chile, ker-*blam!*—en my lan', de chile never move'! My breff mos' hop outer me; en I feel so—so—I doan' know *how* I feel. I crope out, all a-tremblin', en crope aroun' en open de do' easy en slow, en poke my head in behine de chile, sof' en still, en all uv a sudden, I says, *pow!* jis' as loud as I could yell. *She never budge!* Oh, Huck, I bust out a-cryin' en grab her up in my arms, en say, 'Oh de po' little thing! de Lord God Amighty fogive po' ole Jim, kaze he never gwyne to fogive hisself as long's he live!' Oh, she was plumb deef en dumb, Huck, plumb deef en dumb—en I'd ben a-treat'n her so!" (201-02)

We have seen Jim to be a man who can forgive others, but he cannot forgive himself for an unknowingly misguided act. He does not seek to displace blame and responsibility someplace else: on whites, on fate. Every reader, regardless of ethnicity, experiences recognition and acknowledgment in this chapter. Despite the fact that Jim expresses himself with "substandard" English, despite having boxed 'Lizabeth's ears, despite having been on a raft with two rogues who have reenslaved him, Jim transcends his marginality; he is much more than "half-a-man." He is above the South. Huck can now make his affirming statement that Jim must care for his family as much as white people do for theirs: not a racist statement, as opponents of the book have alleged, but rather a racial awakening by Huck as Jim eclipses Huck's own Pap. It is a statement that denies one of the ugliest and most pervasive and pernicious stereotypes encouraged by slavemasters.

Next follows the section often cited by *Huckleberry Finn* opponents as being the most clearly racist passage in the midsection of the novel. Although the chapter focuses primarily on the rogues and the introduction of the Wilks daughters, it begins with the decision to put Jim in disguise so that he can remain alone on the raft during the day with freedom of movement. The resulting burlesque of Shakespeare's *King Lear* and *Othello* provides humor on the surface but at the same time reminds the reader of the precariousness of Jim's position. Jim tells the duke that the ropes used to present him during the day as a runaway slave are "mighty heavy and tiresome" (203). Consistent with his life of costumed disguises and masks, the duke masks Jim in an elaborate disguise. Recounting the scene here is important for the sake of opponents who see this section as an ending of Jim's development in the novel: "He dressed Jim up in a King Lear's outfit—it was a long curtain-calico gown, and a white horse-hair wig and whiskers; and then he took his theatre-paint and painted Jim's face and hands and ears and neck all over a dead dull solid blue, like a man that's been drownded nine days. Blamed if he warn't the horriblest looking outrage I ever see. Then the duke took and wrote out a sign on a shingle so—*Sick Arab— but harmless when not out of his head*" (203-04). According to Huck, "Jim was satisfied. He said it was a sight better than laying tied a couple of years every day and trembling all over every time there was a sound" (204). The grotesque makeover with blue paint and the sign proclaiming Jim to be an Arab assures all concerned that Jim will not be harmed, or even questioned, by passers-by when left alone on the raft. Distortion and perversion make for convincing identity in this society: in this way, the disguise foreshadows Tom Sawyer's work in the final twelve chapters. Huck says, "The duke told him to make himself free and easy, and if anybody ever come meddling around, he must hop out of the wigwam, and carry on a little, and fetch a howl or two like a wild beast, and he reckoned they would light out and leave him alone. Which was sound enough judgment; but you take the average man, and he wouldn't wait for him to howl. Why, he didn't only look like he was dead, he looked considerable more than that" (204). In a novel where extravagant disguise and fascination with robbers, bandits, and Arabs is the norm, Jim's camouflage is not a subtle racist ploy to undermine his character. On the contrary, it is a caricature of it.

Jim continues to construct his own narrative. It is he who expresses the need for another plan to conceal him during the day. His allusion to each day of being tied up feeling like years recalls in the minds of African American readers images of the Middle Passage, the auction block, and the numerous captured runaways, while also anticipating Jim's experience on the Phelps plantation. Once more, opponents to this section must be probed: Just how is it that Twain is negatively portraying Jim? How is he completely marginalized? If Jim's goal is to find a way that better suits him for remaining on the raft alone, his actions can be understood, given that the men with whom he and Huck must negotiate are themselves rogues. Jim never removes his eyes from the ultimate prize—freedom—even for a short time of comfort. His persistence says much in Jim's favor, not against him.

Twain leaves Jim for a time on the raft and sends Huck ashore again with the duke and king. Jim is not with him now, but the lessons Huck has learned from him are reflected in the interaction with the Wilks sisters and other slaves and slave families. Readers have the chance to see that Huck's growth is not dependent on Jim's presence.

In Chapters 26–28 Twain charts Huck's development and compels readers to take notice of just how much he has learned. Huck is now willing to extend himself to act—from his discussion with Joanna, in which he assumes the mask of English servant, to his observing the relationship between the sisters and their slaves, to the slave auction sponsored by the duke and king, to Huck's decision to reveal the elaborate plot and rid himself and Jim once and for all of the two.

While having supper with Joanna Wilks, Huck engages in a discussion on American slavery and European servants. Burlesque and parody allow Huck to voice ironically the difference between being considered a person if you are a slave in the South as opposed to being a nobody if you are a servant in England. This conversation reveals, too, the irony and myth of beneficent slavery. This discussion, juxtaposed to Mary Jane's and Susan's admonishing Joanna for her mistreatment of Huck, further dramatizes Twain's theme. Just as Huck had to apologize to Jim for making him feel ashamed, Joanna must apologize to Huck, as a servant. Mary Jane says to Joanna: "If you was in his place, it would make you feel ashamed; and so you oughtn't to say a thing to another person that will make *them* feel ashamed. . . . The thing is for you to treat him *kind*, and not be saying things to make him remember he ain't in his own country and amongst his own folks" (225). The distinction made here rests on color and being foreign. That the Wilks girls do not think of "their" slave family in the same humane terms they afford Huck must not be lost on the audience.

Huck is once more confronted with the contradiction of his cultural beliefs when the duke and king arrange to sell the slaves of the Wilks girls, a climax to Huck's growing recognition of the humanity of slaves. The emotion, brutality, and sincere feeling that Huck observes during the slave auction not only cause him to act but also cause him and the audience to think of Jim and his family.[13] Huck says of separating the family:

I thought them poor girls and them niggers would break their hearts for grief; they cried around each other, and took on so it most made me down sick to see it. . . . I can't ever get it out of my memory, the sight of them poor miserable girls and niggers hanging around each other's necks and crying; and I reckon I couldn't a stood it all but would a had to bust out and tell on our gang if I hadn't knowed the sale warn't no account and the niggers would be back in a week or two. (234)

We cannot be certain that Twain ever experienced an auction while growing up, but he did have an occasion to see slaves being moved to auction: "I have no recollection of ever seeing a slave auction in that town; but I am suspicious that that is because the thing was a common and commonplace spectacle, not an uncommon and impressive one. I vividly remember seeing a dozen black men and women chained to one another, once, and lying in a group on the pavement, awaiting shipment to the Southern slave market. Those were the saddest faces I have ever seen. Chained slaves could not have been a common sight or this picture would not have made so strong and lasting an impression upon me" (30). That strong impression on Huck—and Twain—comes to a crucial juncture in Chapter 31. Most important here is that the feeling of love between blacks and whites show Huck's readiness to move to action.

Critics agree that this chapter demonstrates Huck's maturation. The first step in this two-part process was for Huck to experience the sudden loss of Jim's presence. Although many have protested Jim's absence during earlier portions of the novel, Chapter 31 is the first time since Jackson's Island that Huck has been completely and wholly separated from Jim. Even with the Grangerfords, Jim, although he is not physically seen, is discovered as a presence at the appropriate time. When the duke and the king decide to use the fake runaway slave bill to sell Jim, this separation is definitely different in tone and potential. Huck must confront the primary issue on which the novel rests, namely, What price freedom? "I went to the raft," he says, "and set down in the wigwam to think. But I couldn't come to nothing. I thought till I wore my head sore, but I couldn't see no way out of the trouble. After all this long journey, and after all we'd done for them scoundrels, here was it all come to nothing, everything all busted up and ruined, because they could have the heart to serve Jim such a trick as that, and make him a slave again all his life, and amongst strangers, too, for forty dirty dollars" (269). As with the Wilks family, the rights of a human being—an African American, have become a matter of "heart."

Huck comes to an initial realization that, given the present circumstances, "as long as he'd *got* to be a slave" (269), Jim would be better off to go back to Miss Watson. In this solution, too, lies *another* problem for the concerned adolescent. Here he must engage the final idol of truth, the rightness of slavery itself. The role Huck will have to assume, not play but assume, if Jim were going to be a free man must now be defined in his new maturity: "And then think of *me*! It would get all around, that Huck Finn helped a nigger to get his freedom; and if I was ever to see anybody from that town again, I'd be ready to get down and lick his boots for shame. That's just the way: a person does a low-down thing, and then he don't want to take no consequences of it. Thinks as long as he can hide it, it ain't no disgrace. That was my fix exactly" (270). The "fix" of every adolescent, black or white, is whether to rebel against control and accept the consequences or to accept and obey, thus compromising independence. What reader in our society can ignore such a double bind?

Once again Huck must take time to deliberate his actively working to free a runaway slave, just as earlier it had taken him fifteen minutes to decide to break another social taboo by humbling himself to a nigger. The mental battle is not easily won. Huck naturally falls back on his previous training from Miss Watson and the widow. But when that training does not help him make up his mind, he prays for guidance, only then realizing the falsity and emptiness of the guidance he thinks he seeks. As he remembers his experiences with Jim, the true meaning of Christian faith, loyalty, and love emerge:

I felt good and all washed clean of sin for the first time I had ever felt so in my life, and I knowed I could pray now. But I didn't do it straight off, but laid the paper down and set there thinking—thinking how good it was that all this happened so, and how near I came to being lost and going to hell. And went on thinking. And got to thinking over our trip down the river; and I see Jim before me, all the time, in the day and in the night-time, sometimes moonlight, sometimes storms, and we a floating along, talking, and singing, and laughing. But somehow I couldn't seem to strike no places to harden me against him, but only the other kind. I'd see him standing my watch on top of his'n, stead of calling me, so I could go on sleeping; and see him how glad he was when I come back out of the fog; and when I come to him again in the swamp, up there where the feud was; and such-like times; and would always call me honey, and pet me, and do everything he could think of for me, and how good he always was; and at last I struck the time I saved him by telling the men we had small-pox aboard, and he was so grateful, and said I was the best friend old Jim ever had in the world, and the *only* one he's got now; and then I happened to look around, and see that paper. . . .

I was a trembling, because I'd got to decide, forever, betwixt two things, and I knowed it. I studied a minute, sort of holding my breath, and then says to myself:

"All right, then, I'll *go* to hell"—and tore it up. (271-72)

The midsection of the novel concludes with this cosmic reversal. A linguistic irony deposes southern heritage and its dislocated piety in favor of an ideal arising solely from the black slave's action—his proof of himself as a whole man. Huck decides to act, a decision that in his mind damns his soul to everlasting hellfire. Talking with students around the country, I find it necessary to explain the significance and lasting impact that language held for the nineteenth century. Today's youth—and some adults as well—see language as something impermanent and temporal. They can say whatever they want and think nothing of the consequences or the affects of frivolous usage on their audience. But Huck's line, "All right, then, I'll *go* to hell," is completely earnest. Think, I ask audiences of all ages and ethnicities, really think about a literal heaven and a literal hell. Whether they are believers or not, Huck is, and we must view this scene from his perspective.

There is no reprieve, no appeal from hell; once in, one is there forever, for eternity, and forever is a long time.

Given the scope of this decision, for whom or for what would they be willing to go to hell, I then ask students. Just as they could not say that they would follow the example of the free northern professor, who goes South and meets Pap Finn on the main street, most have no answer for this question, given Huck's parameters. Until readers examine this section carefully and acknowledge Huck's dilemma from his perspective, the tremendous sacrifice of this scene is lost, and so is its triumph. Not only are they lost in this scene but in its parallel scenes in Chapters 40 and 42, in which Jim must answer "What price freedom?" Few critics have addressed these scenes as parallel, but the continuity is clear. Huck makes a focused decision to sacrifice his eternal Soul, thereby responding to the question of the cost of freedom. Jim, too, must confront this dilemma. Like Huck, he will ultimately place his desire for freedom below the safety of another human being, in this case Tom Sawyer. What price freedom for Jim? His sacrifice so that Tom Sawyer stays alive. What a model for us, all of us, black or white.

Whah Is de Glory?

The (Un)Reconstructed South

All the experiences of the central section have prepared Huck for the final conflict, his decision to free Jim from being made a slave "again all his life . . . amongst strangers . . . for forty dirty dollars" (269). With that resolution, Huck casts off his old cultural beliefs and embraces new ones that feel right. Having watched Huck grow, we know that this decision is not predicated on whether freeing is convenient or comfortable. But the bitter satire of the human condition in final section of the novel impels many readers to ask if its hero is a racist. The new perspective we have on Huck and Jim leads to the answer.

When Huck meets up with Tom Sawyer, the young man who in Huck's eyes personifies intelligence and knowledge, Huck resumes his secondary, supporting role. Huck's deference to Tom in the effort to extricate Jim occurs only after he has tried, as a true friend, to warn Tom not to damn his soul as he, Huck, has done.

A scene that has caused great concern and discussion initiates us into the closure of the novel: Huck's explaining to Aunt Sally why he was delayed in arriving at the Phelps Farm and why he arrives in the manner that he does. Aunt Sally herself supplies the format for Huck to construct his deception when she says, "What's kep' you?—boat get aground?" (279). Huck realizes the need for a convincing story and that he must now come up with a new idea:

"It warn't the grounding—that didn't keep us back but a little. We blowed out a cylinder-head."

"Good gracious! anybody hurt?"

"No'm. Killed a nigger."

"Well, it's lucky; because sometimes people do get hurt." (280)

No one better represents the opposition to this section than Bernard Bell: "[T]he author and his protagonist are kindred spirits in their ambivalence about the humanity and equality of blacks. In response, for example, to the tarring and feathering of the Duke and King, the comic confidence men, Huck is moved to sympathy for them in Chapter 33 .... Yet, earlier when Aunt Sally Phelps asked if anybody was hurt on the boat . . . , Huck's insensitivity to the humanity of blacks . . . is as ironically racist as hers .... Twain, like Huck, was a racist; yet both found themselves fighting nobly, though futilely, against the customs and laws of white supremacy" (135). I agree that Huck's compassion emerges when he sees the duke and king tarred and feathered, and what we subsequently hear are Huck's true feelings without the constrictive disguise that he has donned in order to effect the rescue of Jim. We are inside his mind, listening to his thoughts, thoughts no one but the reader knows. But Bell's argument of insensitivity is perverse. The ironic racism is deceptive coloring for Huck. No reasonable reader misses this. For the reader, it is an utter condemnation through satire of bigotry. Huck is manipulative, and the satire is derived from his knowledge of what would work most effectively to mislead someone who believes in slavery—now his cosmic enemies in the battle between heaven and hell. Twain's double emphasis on the line, by having Aunt Sally repeat part of it, is an obvious authorial indicator of Twain's intention of highlighting the moment.

The Aunt Sally scene is quite different, however, in that we have access to Huck's thoughts only when he is determining what he must do and say in order to disarm and persuade Aunt Sally that he is who he says he is. When he speaks, he says not what is inside his mind but what she expects him to say, and the verisimilitude of the fiction retains its continuity and cohesion. What else could we expect from a work of realism? We have been inside his mind and soul in Chapter 31. We know that he has committed his all to what he believes is the morally, spiritually, and ethically right action, and, make no mistake, Huck does consciously decide to take action. Here too his decision is costly, for with it he faces the possibility of incarceration, branding, various amputations, most certain social ostracizing, and even death. Having seen Huck answer the ultimate question of the price of freedom, it is difficult to imagine wanting a euphemism now. What we get is what we do want: a visionary joke, a larger irony than any that has gone before in this comedy.

In Chapter 16 when Jim spoke of securing "an Ab'litionist to go and steal [his wife and children out of bondage]" (124), Huck's reaction was shock and dismay. He saw such talk as lowering Jim. Compare that scene with this one in Chapter 33, and we find that Huck Finn himself is the "ab'litionist," who will secure Jim's freedom at the price of his very soul. His solicitude for Tom might delude an unwary reader into doubting Huck's sincerity; it should not. The racial slur "nigger" again in no way diminishes what Twain is accomplishing here, for we must ask why Huck is relying once more on this term. What we find on close examination is that, like Jim, Huck is donning the appropriate mask to suit the situation, which requires using the expected language.

Twain reveals in this final section of the novel the true nature of the (un)reconstructed South as represented by Tom Sawyer. Although Huck Finn is no longer the same Huck we met at the novel's beginning, Tom is the same Tom. We know that Tom is still the same mythic, Romantic's Romantic, in love with perceived adventure rather than with the unorchestrated events of the real world. The real world is the one in which Jim has always existed and in which Huck and Jim both exist after they embark on the river. Unlike them, Tom has remained in stasis throughout the narrative, offstage except when, by proxy, his ideas bring Huck and Jim into danger. Twain attacks Tom's mental attitude early and late from the direct frontal criticism of Scott in *Life on the Mississippi* to covert sallies in virtually every other work in the canon. Twain's books never favor the tutors in chivalry and suspense. Twain reveals this predisposition to the reader again when Huck tells Tom his plan to free Jim. About to respond, Tom stops in midsentence, almost revealing that Jim is already free. A special perversity is represented by the fact that he lies through this blatant omission to his best friend, Huck, a friend who admires and respects Tom's mind and humanity. Could the rest of the action he controls be any less perverse?

The reading audience sometimes fails to observe that it is not Huck who initiates and plays the game of let's free the free nigger; it is Tom Sawyer. Should the reader, particularly the African American, condemn Huck for not taking the lead in this elaborate and dangerous plan and for yielding control to Tom? It is not Huck who deduces Jim's location in the hut by the ash-hopper; it is Tom. Although both see food being taken to the hut, only Tom connects the contents of the dinner to Jim. Twain the ironist is at work. The key element for Tom is the stereotypical watermelon. Huck assumes that the slave is feeding a dog, but Tom reminds him that dogs do not eat watermelon. Huck says, "So it was—I noticed it. Well, it does beat all, that I never thought about a dog not eating watermelon. It shows how a body can see and don't see at the same time" (293). Huck expresses later in Chapter 34 that he knows Tom to be extremely intelligent: "What a head for a boy to have! If I had Tom Sawyer's head, I wouldn't trade it off to be a duke, nor mate of a steamboat, nor clown in a circus, nor nothing I can think of. I went to thinking out a plan [of escape for Jim], but only just to be doing something; I knowed very well where the right plan was going to come from" (294). The dominant figure and the dominant culture dominate.

Reprising three moments in the action where Tom was absent, Huck concludes that he will rely on this seemingly masterful ally and leader. Yet it will be an uneasy alliance. Huck has always felt that because of Tom's great propensity for reading, he possesses the expertise to execute important undertakings. Logic dictates to Huck that he yield to the person with the greatest chance for success. The ultimate irony here is Huck's self-perception of intellectual weakness. Huck may not notice such minute details as the watermelon, but he can and does keenly observe human nature. What Huck has learned on the river, as well as in his life with Pap and the widow and Miss Watson, has produced in him a capacity of understanding which is far richer in insight than Tom's. His wisdom derives from his bond with Jim.

In the last chapters, Huck's and Jim's wisdom for expression will struggle against great odds, as Twain intends. Huck utters substantive social comments as his sight and insight improve because of Jim's influence over the course of their adventures. His yielding to Tom is not a capitulation or a conscious burlesquing of a serious matter at Jim's expense. Instead it is an attempt to keep to the oath he makes earlier. One of the most saddening portions of this section is rarely mentioned by critics—Huck's firm faith in Tom's sincerity:

Well, one thing was dead sure; and that was, that Tom Sawyer was in earnest and was actuly going to help steal that nigger out of slavery. That was the thing that was too many for me. Here was a boy that was respectable, and well brung up; and had a character to lose; and folks at home that had characters; and he was bright and not leather-headed; and knowing and not ignorant; and not mean, but kind; and yet here he was, without any more pride, or rightness, or feeling, than to stoop to this business, and make himself a shame, and his family a shame, before everybody. I *couldn't* understand it, no way at all. . . . I knowed I ought to just jump up and tell him so; and so be his true friend, and let him quit the whole thing right where he was, and save himself. (295)

In this important section Twain exposes the distorted underpinnings of a society whose implacable truths have been contradicted throughout the novel. Tom Sawyer—the (un)reconstructed South—relies on and perverts every concept on which the South presumably structured its mythic persona: pride, rightness, filial loyalty, honesty, and salvation. In comparison with Jim's defining moment with Huck on true friendship, Twain creates for the audience a stark, undeniable contrast. Huck's emphasis here recalls the essence of his and Jim's real relationship as developed in the "trash" incident, Jim's calling after Huck, and Huck's own great reprise. True friendship has been successfully redefined by Twain as lying across racial boundaries—the only real solution to the Jim dilemma. Tom's way is now a travesty, by design.

Some critics, such as Henry Nash Smith in "A Sound Heart and a Deformed Conscience," cite Huck's decision to accept Tom Sawyer's aid as a weakness both in Huck's character and in the novel's structure. Others complain that Huck in this passage begins to reveal signs of relenting in his efforts and sincerity. Their mistake is in hating the action without being able to see that Twain distances it from the actor. Huck must be shown dealing with the last vestige of what he deems to be sacrosanct and above reproach. He has abandoned unreflecting support of slavery because of his experiences with Jim. He has already made an overwhelming decision for himself. But Huck is a boy, not a social theorist: we could not expect him to allow his best friend to place his soul in jeopardy without any demur. Nor has he the cynicism of an adult capable of penetrating Tom's mystifying behavior, so he accepts his "help" without recognizing, as we the readers do, the element of insincerity on which it is based. Twain fully expresses this point through Huck's extended statement of surprise. This passage also shows us how Huck really views himself. Critics such as Smith have concluded that Huck, because of his low self-esteem, has very little to lose. Is that assertion accurate? Is not one's soul the ultimate loss, no matter how poor, how uneducated, how classless? It would appear that Twain is speaking directly to the audience here, as well, through the honest words and concerns of an adolescent who is trying to figure out what it all means when beliefs are turned inside out not once but, now, twice. Smith has missed the point. And so, Huck, the true and sincere friend, must at least try to save his companion, Tom, from the "sure" fate of eternal damnation. Tom, of course, knowing that no such fate awaits him, plays the intelligent hero who dares to risk all to help his friends. So begins the great travesty of freeing the free slave. Tom's role is monstrous and insincere, truly an "evasion"; Huck, now more a son of Jim than of Pap, is true to his and Jim's humanity outside the law. Such fidelity was easy as melodramatic events propelled the story; it is very complex in the burlesque framework now established.

Jim, of course, assumes a primary role in this escapade. Critics from Marx, Booth, and Bell to Peaches Henry have indicted the closing chapters as tremendously weak. Henry, for example, claims that any strides Jim may have reached by the final section of the novel, still leave him a "stereotypical, superstitious 'darky' that Twain's white audience would have expected and in which they would have delighted" (33). Continuing with this misperception, she describes Jim as one who "darkens the closing chapters of the novel." She goes on to note, "Regardless of Twain's motivation or intent, Jim does deflate and climb back into the minstrel costume. His self-respect and manly pursuit of freedom bow subserviently before the childish pranks of an adolescent white boy" (38).

But previous chapters have shown us that Twain relies on parody and burlesque along with Jim's masterful language manipulation to convey mental attitudes toward freedom, equity, voice, and family. Each character must maintain the character that society has caused him to represent even though it may be different from what he has become. Tom Sawyer must metonymically represent the slave-holding South, that of the forced (un)reconstructed South. That is verisimilitude. Huck Finn must maintain the attitude of the reconstructing southerner. That is Twain's vision. Jim must maintain his mask for self-preservation and his linguistic manipulation as protection. That is verisimilitude. Anything else would have transformed Jim's dialogue and actions into those of an unrecognizable Romantic hero. While that is Jim's tragedy, it is also why blacks as well as whites can feel the novel's greatness.

Signs of Twain's intent are manifold. When Jim assesses his situation and sees that Huck is acting in concert with Tom Sawyer, he shifts his language. Terms of subserviency—"Mars Tom," "Misto Tom," and "sah"—are suddenly prominent. Has Jim forgotten or lost his taste for freedom and family? Is this not the same man who steadily eyed Huck and called him "trash?" Is this not the man who advised Huck that their "royalty" on the raft were nothing but rogues? Opponents constantly ask where his voice is now and assert that Jim reassumes his previous slave invisibility and silence.

When Tom's inventions exceed pragmatics, as Jim understands the situation, he refuses to engage in that part of the evasion—the severing of limbs, placing of spiders in the cabin, placing of rattlesnakes, and planting flowers and watering them with tears. Of this section Harold Beaver, in his essay "Run, Nigger, Run," articulates most succinctly the general problem:

> Jim is merely a good nigger: good humored, simple (with the king and duke), improvident (with his financial investments), kind-hearted (to Huck), displaying a contented African patience with a physical endurance that might have proved fatal to anyone except an African. The stress throughout is not on his trances or voodoo potency so much as on his ability to: preserve an equilibrium between true Negro optimism, as a Southerner would have put it, and African fatalism. So much Huck could observe. The inherent shrewdness was not so conspicuous. For Jim rarely speaks out. (188)

Jim's "good humor" involves insisting that he "doan' skasely ever cry" (331), a comment as misleading as Huck's earlier comment that he didn't take any stock in dead people. His simplicity with the duke and king involved his testing them and rejecting them. His improvidence, in fact, with "stock" was a poignant fact of his life and of all investments, as any reader of the *Wall Street Journal* today can attest. To degrade Jim's character by labeling it "true negro optimism, as a Southerner would have put it," is to take a stance which is ambivalent in itself, although probably not intended to be perversely racist or critically unaware. Jim's "African fatalism," possibly in reference to the "luck" sentiments as expressed in passing Cairo, is totally uncharacteristic of him at any time in the novel. Finally, Jim speaks out not "rarely" but many times, in fact, both to Huck and to Tom.

While otherwise offering valuable analysis, when Beaver uses the word "merely," it is clear that he has badly missed the heroism in Jim's behavior. Jim speaks out as the situation warrants. He is not so foolish as to have his say at the expense of compromising the situation. He never forgets, though, that he is still in the South, he has been captured as a runaway, and he is without his passport and stalwart friend, Huck. Only an inept melodramatist would have given his character a formal set-speech on racism and recapture; it seems spurious to suggest or imply such an alternative as a critical point.

Jim initially does argue with Tom as he had with Huck, one of the best of these attempts being the glory scene in Chapter 38. Tom, the orchestrator of the great escape, admonishes Jim:

"Jim, don't act so foolish. A prisoner's *got* to have some kind of a dumb pet, and if a rattlesnake hain't ever been tried, why, there's more glory to be gained in your being the first to ever try it than any other way you could ever think of to save your life."

"Why, Mars Tom, I doan' *want* no sich glory. Snake take 'n bite Jim's chin off, den *whah* is de glory? No, sah, I doan' want no sich doin's. . . ."

"Mars Tom, I's willin' to tackle mos' anything 'at ain't onreasonable, but ef you en Huck fetches a rattlesnake in heah for me to tame, I's gwyne to *leave,* dat's *shore.*" (328-29)

No voice? Jim says what he must, when he must. But he also realizes that the equation has changed with Tom Sawyer in it. Tom, a representative of the (un)reconstructed South, barely sees or hears Jim as a real person. Jim can afford to say only so much in front him. This much is clear at the end of the chapter when Huck explains that Tom has heard too much of Jim's voice:

Jim said he would "jis' 's soon have tobacker in his coffee"; and found so much fault with it, and with the work and bother of raising the mullen, and jews-harping the rats, and petting and flattering up the snakes and spiders and things, on top of all the other work he had to do on pens, and inscriptions, and journals, and things, which made it more trouble and worry and responsibility to be a prisoner than anything he ever undertook, that Tom most lost all patience with him; and said he was just loadened down with more gaudier chances than a prisoner ever had in the world to make a name for himself, and yet he didn't know enough to appreciate them, and they was just about wasted on him. So Jim he was sorry, and said he wouldn't behave so no more. (331-32)

Jim readjusts his mask so that it fits more closely, apologizes, and promises to behave more appropriately in the future. In comedy we must now endure the undoing of the truths Huck and Jim developed in isolation. With Tom in the picture, Huck and Jim have again become social beings.

Twain never allows the reader or Huck to forget the danger of the situation, even though the "evasion" is indeed a burlesque. Having given us a visceral sense of lynching in the Sherburn episode, Twain presents a second and third lynch mob. Because of the note Tom leaves detailing a plot to steal Jim from the Phelps farm, a lynching party is formed as a "posse." Tom thought this response would provide ample decoy for them so that they could escape without notice. Tom's note of warning inverts Huck's moral reasoning in respect to Jim, and the outcome is grotesque. Tom writes that although he has been part of the plot to steal Jim, he has now found "relligion and wish[es] to quit it and lead a honest life again, and will betray the helish design" (338). As Tom plans, the men and dogs gather, sixteen men and twenty-two dogs. Whereas the mob that sought Colonel Sherburn fascinated and frightened Huck, here he is no mere observer. The spectacle this time makes him so ill that he has to sit. Tom, Huck, and Jim escape with the mob literally at their heels, and Tom is shot in the leg.

Many opponents of the novel have difficulty with how the characters respond. After realizing that their escape has been a resounding success and that Jim is a free man, Huck says: "*Now*, old Jim, you're a free man *again*, and I bet you won't ever be a slave no more" (344). Jim, although he has complained about the apparent trials and tribulations of this escape, also realizes that Tom has delivered on his promise. Their faith in Tom was properly placed, degrading though it was. In this respect, Tom accomplishes more than the region he represents accomplished as an integrated "new South."

But Twain pushes us into a second reversal so rapidly that we race past this point. Tom has been injured, and Jim and Huck's rejoicing quickly ends. The pair turn their immediate attention and concern to Tom. How characteristic of these two, as we have come to know them! Opponents have asserted that it is not incumbent upon Jim to sacrifice here the very thing for which he has been questing since the narrative's beginning. Some critics, particularly African American parents, cite this scene as especially racist because Twain describes Jim as relinquishing his freedom for a white boy who really does not have his best interest at heart to begin with. After all, Tom knows the truth of Jim's manumission. To this reading audience Jim becomes an Uncle Tom, and Twain seems to show his true racist colors.

But we must believe all that has happened in the novel up to this point. We have been exhilarated with Jim's evolution in previous chapters. We believed Huck's ultimate sacrifice. These characters represent a vision with which we have begun to identify because we have seen intimately their loyalty, their faith, their honesty, their naivete, their fortitude, and their self-reliance. How could Jim have done anything but what he did? It is exactly what we expect of him as the man, the free man, the husband, and the father we know him to be. It is not Twain who empowers Jim; rather, it is Jim the fully rounded character who empowers himself to risk sacrificing his freedom for what he feels to be right. Huck and he discuss the situation:

But me and Jim was consulting—and thinking. And we'd thought a minute, I says:

"Say it, Jim."

So he says:

"Well, den, dis is de way it look to me, Huck. Ef it wuz *him* dat 'uz bein' sot free, en one er de boys wuz to git shot, would he say, 'Go on en save me, nemmine 'bout a doctor f'r to save dis one?' Is dat like Mars Tom Sawyer? Would he say dat? You *bet* he wouldn't! *Well*, den, is *Jim* gwyne to say it? No sah—I doan' budge a step out'n dis place, 'dout a *doctor*; not if it's forty year!" (345)

Can readers miss the number forty, recalling the forty dirty dollars that brought Jim back to captivity? Twain's choice of words like "consulting" and, recalling and reversing Tom's earlier "studying," "thinking" remind us that Jim acts in contrast to Tom's incorrectly formed sense of humanity. As with the verbal battles in the novel's first third, Jim prepares for Huck an argument with the deduction that Huck, knowing Jim, anticipates. Note, however, that Jim does not say that he will not continue to seek his freedom. He simply says that he will not leave Tom alone without help. It might even be argued that hostile critics miss the fact that Jim, as Twain's spokesman, is so powerful because he is not a racist or an absolutist. Recognizing a heroic standard of behavior, he adheres to it, whether white or black. This important distinction is often overlooked. Jim truly comes to parity with the other characters through this last great heroic logomachy, and Tom Sawyer will respond in kind, in awakening from his delirium, to cry that Jim is as "free as any cretur that walks this earth" (360).

While Jim is called an Uncle Tom for his decision in this scene, Huck's reaction has Twain opponents calling him racist: "I knowed he was white inside, and I reckoned he'd say what he did say—so it was all right, now, and I told Tom I was a-going for a doctor. . . . Jim was to hide in the woods when he see the doctor coming, till he was gone again" (345-46). Twain highlights the irony of the moment by reinforcing our false assumption that whites are the setters of morals. Is Huck's racism emerging in his saying that Jim is white inside? Yes, Huck still has much to learn about race. But the travesty of moral color is a direct response to those Americans who persist even now to see one race as morally degraded.

As a point of comparison, we might explore another brand of racism. William Lloyd Garrison once advised Frederick Douglass that he needed to speak more like a southern slave and less like a white man or an educated northern colored person (Douglass). Douglass, of course, ignored the advice and continued to speak as he chose. Like many other African Americans, I have vivid memories of my family being accused by other African Americans of trying to be white or thinking we were white because of how we spoke, behaved, and thought. Was Garrison a racist? Were the African American children and adults who berated other African Americans racists? Some believe that people of color cannot be racist. I disagree with that as much as I disagree with Twain opponents who assert that Huck's calling Jim "white" shows his racism. As I mentioned earlier, a student many years ago asked me whether Huck at the novel's conclusion is a racist. I told that student then, and I reassert now, that Huck can never look at another individual of African American descent without being affected by his experience of Jim as well as the other African Americans he encounters in this novel. Is he a racist? No. Can we presume that a long course of development will have to take place before his voice no longer shows its southern origin? Sadly, yes. Twain is a realist.

Of all that happens in the novel, the scene in Chapter 42 is perhaps the most troubling because it is so very realistic. After experiencing the traumas of the "great escape," Tom's being shot, and the recapture, Jim must yet endure southern vilification and brutality: "They cussed Jim considerble, though, and give him a cuff or two, side the head, once in a while, but Jim never said nothing, and he never let on to know me, and they took him to the same cabin, and put his own clothes on him, and chained him again . . . and chained his hands, too, and both legs, and said he warn't to have nothing but bread and water to eat" (356). Jim's humanity and his presence reveal themselves once again, this time through the doctor. The doctor must admit to the mob that despite the fact that Jim is a runaway slave he came out of hiding when the doctor needed help in removing the bullet from Tom's leg. It is at this point that the audience bears witness to Jim's ultimate decision. He knows that the doctor will not let him go, but he chooses to do what he feels is morally right anyway.

Although some critics have seen this scene, and others before it, as attenuating Jim's character, verbal irony in the doctor's speech to the mob diminishes not Jim as much as those around him, for it is they, including the doctor, a man who professes to live by the Hippocratic oath, who lack humanity. En masse, they represent the destructive and hypocritical Southern mindset that Jim and Huck have encountered in their symposium down the river. The mob's response after hearing from the doctor about Jim's unquestionable humanity adds that parodic satiric spice that pervades this novel. Again, it is Huck on whom nothing is lost, not even the unfairness of their treatment of Jim:

Then the others softened up a little, too, and I was mighty thankful to that old doctor for doing Jim that good turn; and I was glad it was according to my judgment of him, too; because I thought he had a good heart in him and was a good man, the first time I see him. Then they all agreed that Jim had acted very well, and was deserving to have some notice took of it, and reward. So every one of them promised, right out and hearty, that they wouldn't cuss him no more.

Then they come out and locked him up. I hoped they was going to say he could have one or two of the chains took off, because they was rotten heavy, or could have meat and greens with his bread and water, but they didn't think of it, and I reckoned it warn't best for me to mix in, but I judged I'd get the doctor's yarn to Aunt Sally, somehow or other, as soon as I'd got through the breakers that was laying just ahead of me. (358)

Is Jim supposed to be visible, voiced, and independent before these men? No. If he were, the metaphor Twain has so carefully constructed throughout this narrative would have failed. In fact, Jim's moment of heroism should be obvious to any reader. As Jim is being cussed and cuffed, he "never said nothing, and he never let on to know me." As his loyalty to Tom is absolute, so is his loyalty to Huck. Twain emphasizes his resolutions with three negatives bunched together for impact. In the face of the power of the posse, Jim is steadfast. By relying on unlikely heroes—an adolescent, throw-away boy and an unlettered slave—Twain weaves into this narrative a metaphor compelling the reader to revisit the pain and trauma of this period in America's history and, like Huck, to be transformed. The responses, actions, and interactions of the main characters provide important emblems for readers, regardless of age, ethnicity, class, or epoch. Jim's exceptional humanity, his sacrifice, and his influence on Huck and the reader, as well as his lack of affect on the mob and the Phelpses are the subtle points of metaphor Twain renders. That Huck remains true to his oath and determines how he can use the doctor's yarn to influence Aunt Sally on Jim's behalf completes Twain's message about the failure and yet the untapped potential of the post-Reconstruction period. This section—this allegedly failed section—painfully and carefully depicts the thorny path that African Americans had yet to tread during Twain's own day. Reconstruction had not worked as well for the southern ex-slave as many had anticipated. A slave today, a freedman tonight: what does one do? The "Jim dilemma" which Twain presents to the reader renders one scenario through the visibility and voice of Jim. As we experience Jim, with Huck, with other slaves, as well as with proponents of slavery, we see exactly what the slave as well as the freedman confronted on a daily basis. From a modern perspective *Adventures of*

Huckleberry Finn creates the environment conducive for the reader to observe and learn these historic and contemporary truths from a comfortable distance rather than from an "in your face" point of view.

That Huck cannot understand why Tom goes to so much trouble to "set a free nigger free" has continued to confound his critics. But when we look at the purpose of the kind of satire Twain has chosen to use, could there have been an effective alternative ending? It seems necessary for Twain to have rendered Tom Sawyer's and the Phelpses' mental attitudes, and to do so through parody and satire, through verbal and situational irony, in order to reveal "the relation of the text to the compromising and conditionalizing context of its utterance" (Morson and Emerson 78). It is this parodic style that "historicizes and . . . exposes the conditions that engendered claims of unconditionality" (78). According to Northrop Frye, this kind of satire "[a]t its most concentrated . . . presents us with a vision of the world in terms of a single intellectual pattern. The intellectual structure built up from this story makes for violent dislocations in the customary logic of the narrative" (310). Twain is writing about a character still set within a world that has not gone beyond racism.

Frye continues that the style sometimes results in the reader's mistaken belief that the writer's style and structure are careless. The unfamiliar style and structure require that readers revise their methods of reading a narrative. They may also have to revise their expectations and preconceived notions about the characters. The relationship between the reader, particularly the African American reader, and the novel has been the focus of this discussion, and we have focused as well on the relationship between readers and the African American presences in the novel. Rather than appreciating the masterful linguistic manipulation and strategic arguments with which Twain has endowed the characters, many African American critics of the novel hear and see only "nigger." John Wallace recommends his revised version of the novel, from which such words have been deleted, over the original: "It no longer depicts blacks as inhuman, dishonest, or unintelligent, and it contains a glossary of Twainisms. Most adolescents will enjoy laughing at Jim and Huck in this adaptation" (24). And they will also have a naive, watered-down, and delusive vision of their own and their nation's heritage.

An approach such as Wallace's brings to the front a serious problem facing African Americans today. It is one of (non)recognition and (un)acknowledgement. Today's reading audience itself assumes a mask that precludes any necessity for acknowledging slavery and Jim and the other slaves depicted in the novel. As we have seen, this mask so obscures the vision that readers overlook even the free professor from the North. Let us discard the mask. Let us instead recognize that blacks and whites together must overcome such a problematic hindrance to substantive identification and communication. Shelley Fisher Fishkin takes the position that Jim does gain his voice and never compromises it. If, as opponents assert, the sound of Jim's voice is diminished, it is not because the character fades but because the hope and promise of Reconstruction failed. If we, at the end of the novel feel frustrated with Jim's situation, our feeling is appropriate to the education we have undergone at Twain's hands as to Jim's real integrity of character and moral purpose.

For Twain's painful rendering of the South's inhumanity before and after the Civil War, he relies on parodic satire to convey ambivalence so as to not completely alienate his reader. Morrison says that for the writer "in a wholly racialized society, there is no escape from racially inflected language, and the work writers do to *unhobble the imagination* from the demands of that language is complicated, interesting, and definitive" (*Playing in the Dark* 13; italics added). *Adventures of Huckleberry Finn* accomplishes such an unhobbling by refusing to allow the reader to escape the truth of a horrific period in American history. As Morrison observes, "The agency for Huck's struggle is the nigger Jim, and it is absolutely necessary . . . that the term *nigger* be inextricable from Huck's deliberations about who and what he himself is—or, more precisely, is not. The major controversies about the greatness or near greatness of *Adventures of Huckleberry Finn* as an American (or even 'world') novel exist as controversies because they forego a close examination of the interdependence of slavery and freedom, of Huck's growth and Jim's serviceability within it, and even Mark Twain's inability to continue to explore the journey into free territory" (55). To have avoided using "nigger," "hell," and "poor white trash" would have been a denial, a lie, that would have undermined the novel's power to move readers to frustration at Jim's physical situation.

Twain never meant for this novel to be painless. He uses humor as Jonathan Swift does. He never meant, as Wallace proposes, for readers to only laugh at Jim and Huck. In her essay "What Does 'Nigger' Mean?" novelist Gloria Naylor queries the meaning and impact of using "nigger." She concludes that even if the word were erased totally from the mouths of white society, as in Wallace's adaptation of *Adventures of Huckleberry Finn*, no one can be naive enough to believe that it would disappear from white minds. And, I add, it also would not disappear from African American minds—nor should it. Without the memory of what a word once meant and what it can continue to mean, we as a society are doomed only to repeat earlier mistakes about our-selves, each other, and serious issues involving us all.

Are we beyond needing correctives, as some of the novel's oppo-nents suggest? I think of the literature book I read in high school, which wrote of slavery, "[L]et your imagination re-create the scenes that gave rise to the spirituals: [Negro] men and women picking cot-ton in the fields; men loading heavy bales on barges, with one rich voice singing out the varying lines and the whole company joining in the refrain" (Fadiman 670-72).[1] This picturesque image appeared in the 1958 edition of *Adventures in American Literature*, but it was used in my classroom in the 1970s. No mention of "nigger," "hell," "poor white trash," lynch mobs, dogs, or chains here, yet it strikes me as far more racist than Twain's use of these words to render the trauma, the brutality, the yearning for freedom, and the rationalizations that up-held slavery. I was fortunate in having parents and some discerning teachers who supplemented standard texts like my literature book with other books to read and open discussions about the issues they raised. Without the gift of that, I would have a very different impression of both my people and Euro-Americans. In their wisdom and out of their own courage, they dared me to look, to question, and then finally to write. Among the books they gave me was *Adventures of Huckleberry Finn*.

Notes

Introduction

1. John Wallace again expresses this view in his essay "The Case Against *Huckleberry Finn*," in *Satire or Evasion? Black Perspectives on Huckleberry Finn*.

2. Peaches Henry cites the 1983 Penn State incident in which a committee examined the effects of reading this novel on ninth-grade students ("The Struggle for Tolerance: Race and Censorship in *Huckleberry Finn*"). The finding of the committee was that the novel should remain in the curriculum but should be moved from the ninth grade to the eleventh or twelfth.

3. For a detailed chronicle of attacks on *Adventures of Huckleberry Finn* see Leslie A. Fiedler, "*Huck Finn*: The Book We Love to Hate."

4. Ms. Monterio protested the teaching of Twain's novel, contending that her daughter fell prey to racial harassment and taunting when she and her classmates had to read *Huckleberry Finn* (quoted in Valley).

Ms. Monterio later had to be ejected from a discussion I was leading due to her disruptive behavior. The incident caused me to begin considering: At what point does one parent have the right to hobble not only her own child but the minds and the imaginations of other children as well before those who have custodial care of education assert their voices and concern?

Chapter 1

1. Morrison calls this form of academic sabotage "silence and evasion." According to Morrison this practice has routinely and historically permeated literary criticism: "[I]n matters of race, silence and evasion have historically

ruled literary discourse. Evasion has fostered another, substitute language in which the issues are encoded, foreclosing open debate. The situation is aggravated by the tremor that breaks into discourse on race. It is further complicated by the fact that the habit of ignoring race is understood to be a graceful, even generous, liberal gesture. To notice is to recognize an already discredited difference. . . . According to this logic, every well-bred instinct argues against noticing and forecloses adult discourse" (*Playing in the Dark* 9-10).

2. While debate always rages as to what defines great literature as well as what should be included in a definitive list of works the well-informed reader should know, I personally define great literature in the Aristotelian sense that, first, all discourse is persuasive and, second, effective persuasive discourse moves people to act.

3. Kenneth Burke, in *A Rhetoric of Motives*, explores the relationship between writer and reading audience with the text functioning as umbilical cord and explains that a reader's identification with the narrative and recognition of his changed feelings denotes successful communication. The writer must equip the message with sufficient "identifiable tags" (20-21) so that readers will be able to mark the concepts and ideas being communicated. The ultimate goal, then, is to create an atmosphere conducive to constructive discussion, not the removal of all possible objections.

4. I once taught at a high school where one of the fundraisers was "Slave Day." Several days prior to the actual day, students with forms would solicit each classroom and offer a "slave for a day" at a specific price. At that time I was the only African American teacher, and while no one saw this sale as anything but a fundraiser and innocent fun, I must admit that I viewed it with awe—not because I was insulted or because I thought that they were positing a theory on slavery but because no one seemed to think about the whole premise of slavery, whether the southern kind or that of ancient cultures.

5. To move students into the literal meaning, I have found that placing them in a Middle Passage scenario works extremely well. In this role playing and role reversal, I assume the voices of the colonizers and slave traders, thereby transforming students into slaves from a variety of ethnic groups who were to be first generation New World slaves: Moor, Berber, Ibo, Seke, Yoruba, Asante, Fon, Ewe, Fante, Susu, Mandingo, Fulni, Ga, Gabon. I place them in slave ships like that of John Hawkins's ship *Jesus*, which traveled to Africa in 1562. I verbally recreate for them, with the help of multimedia aids, the cramped conditions, the stench, the lack of privacy, communications, and san-

itary accommodations. On our disembarkation, I "orientate" them to the new roles in this new place. Forcing them to engage their already vivid and three-dimensional imaginations, I explain that whatever they physically own is now mine. I then take away the two unique features that distinguish human kind—their own names and their language. Without a surname, or even a first name, without the power of language, and with the promise that as owner I, and not the biological parents, own any progeny, the students soon realize that they have brought to the narrative very little information about how the southern slave must have felt. It is not long before students begin asking me questions about fairness, expressing dislike for me, and recognizing and acknowledging Jim's situation and definition of freedom.

6. See also Jerry Gafio Watts's *Heroism and the Black Intellectual.*

7. Funded by private donations, the house in Hartford has now become *The Mark Twain House* and functions as a working museum, repository, research, and educational facility.

8. Again, even with this issue I have found students themselves the most demanding, objective, and fair arbiters to determine Twain's racism. Whether or not each student has a room of his or her own, each clearly understands the importance of possessing a space that belongs to him or her. To show them that I understand this necessity on many different levels, I cite my having my own room growing up, my daughter's having her own room, and my study's being my space now. Twain is no different, I explain.

9. In Texas, for example, concerned citizens have pushed for legislation, as a complement to House Bill 1, "Parent Involvement and Education," that would allow parents to censor books deemed unsuitable for students to read. Each approved textbook must be free of language that "refers to one or more specific racial groups and that, in the opinion of the board, considering the context in which the language occurs, is derogatory or malicious and has no educational purpose appropriate to the age of the student. The board shall adopt rules for the implementation of this subsection" (Floor Amendment No. 44G). Senator Royce West attempted to have this piece of legislation passed in 1995 but failed to garner sufficient votes. He decided to introduce the bill again in the January 1997 session of the state legislature, from "a different perspective," according to Senator West's Education Director, Lawanda Barton. Twain's *Adventures of Huckleberry Finn* was the primary catalyst for this bill. For further information about Senator West's position with specific regard to this novel, see Fishkin's book, *Lighting Out for the Territory: Reflections on Mark Twain and American Culture.*

Chapter 2

1. George Schuyler's novels *Black No More* and *Black Empire* as well as his contributions to the *Pittsburgh Courier* (1933–39) all resemble Twain's aggressive and personal style.

2. Ira Berlin's *Slave Without Masters: The Free Negro in the Antebellum South* is an excellent source for exploring the mores and social as well as political beliefs of the South's reaction to the free African Americans.

3. The logomachy, the contentious use of words, reveals more intently and more succinctly character developments. Menippean satires use logomachies for this very effect: Petronius's *The Satyricon*, Rabelais's *The Gargantuan and Pantagruel*, Cervantes's *Don Quixote de La Mancha*, Laurence Sterne's *Tristram Shandy*, Swift's "A Modest Proposal" and "Battle of the Books," Carroll's *Alice in Wonderland* and *Through the Looking Glass* and George Schuyler's *Black No More*.

4. Mallioux discusses the rhetorical strategies Twain uses, but he does not analyze these logomachies from Jim's voice, a voice that I am asserting is always a double voice.

5. The term *syllogism* as it is used here refers to Aristotle's definition in his *Rhetoric*. Aristotle says that a syllogism is a provable scientific fact; Richard Lanham divides the Aristotelian syllogism into three types, the one here being a hypothetical syllogism. This kind of syllogism, according to Lanham, "is composed of an 'if' clause, called the antecedent, and the 'then' clause, called the consequent" (155).

6. Such inescapable and provable logic is syllogistic rather than probable, or enthymematic, another term used by Aristotle.

7. With regard to double-voicing I am relying here on Mikhail Bakhtin's *Problems of Dostoyevsky's Poetics* and *The Formal Method in Literary Scholarship* and Henry Louis Gates's *The Signifying Monkey*. Bakhtin defines double-voicing as speech diversity which is "*another's speech in another's language*, serving to express authorial intentions but in a refracted way. Such speech constitutes a special type of *double-voiced discourse*" (*The Dialogic Imagination* 325). According to Bakhtin, these two voices are "interrelated" in their dialogism and are internalized.

8. Morson discusses this relationship between audience and parodist as an active one in which the parodist *appears* to direct the audience's attention to the surface of what is being said and heard between the speaker and his audience

but is in actuality directing the author's audience to rethink the occasion that caused the statement (Morson and Emerson 71).

9. Zora Neale Hurston captures through the humor of old African American folktales this cardinal rule in *Mules and Men*, a collection of folklore. The story to which I am referring here is "Big Talk" (77-79). While I would not recommend this story for high school students, I would recommend it for their teachers as well as high school parents who understand the humor and style of folk humor.

10. The term *double voice* as used here relies on Bakhtin's definition of parody and double-voicing (*The Dialogic Imagination* 179-76).

11. I am using *trope* as defined in Richard Lanham's *A Handlist of Rhetorical Terms*.

12. While Cooper meticulously takes specific writers to task for not doing more to support their professed convictions, and praises those like Whittier who do, she omits Mark Twain, neither attacking nor praising him. When speaking of the passive American or the racist American, she cites not Twain, but Edgar Allan Poe, as one on whom all abolitionist attention and sense of mission are lost. Cooper, as did Emerson, Melville, Whittier, and Thoreau, wanted a literature that would "catalyze substantive change" (18). Like Twain, theirs was a literature of constant (re)visioning and (re)evaluation, for themselves as well as for their audiences.

Chapter 3

1. This derogatory term was not coined until the twentieth century, according to Clarence Major in *Juba to Jive: A Dictionary of African-American Slang*.

2. In his foreword to Frances Harper's *Iola Leroy* Gates remarks on the relative obscurity of texts by African American women writers: "For reasons unclear to me even today, few of these marvelous renderings of the Afro-American woman's consciousness were reprinted in the late 1960s and early 1970s, when so many other texts of the Afro-American literary tradition were resurrected from the dark and silent graveyard of the out-of-print and were reissued in facsimile editions aimed at the hungry readership for canonical texts in the nascent field of black studies."

3. For a detailed discussion see Shelley Fisher Fishkin's "Jerry" in *Was Huck*

Black? Mark Twain and African-American Voices, as well as David L. Smith's "Huck, Jim, and American Racial Discourse."

4. The term *trickster figure* is used here as Henry Louis Gates, Jr., uses it in *The Signifying Monkey: A Theory of Afro-American Literary Criticism.* The term is also employed by Smith, Fishkin, and Abrahams.

5. He so angered some that an article in the *New-York Gazette* called him "a sooty scoundrel" (January 1839, vol.1, no.2).

6. Compare this description of the "appropriate" library with that as described by Samuel E. Cornish in *The Colored American* (17 July 1838) and then by David Ruggles in *The Colored American* (August 1838).

7. The Compromise of 1850, also known as the Clay Compromise, set the pace for continuing slavery and consequently strengthened the Fugitive Slave Act of 1793 by allowing federal officials to capture and return slaves who escaped from slave-holding states. This measure was energetically supported by Daniel Webster and denounced by Ralph Waldo Emerson. Emerson states, "Was there nothing better for the foremost American man to tell his countrymen than that slavery was now at that strength that they must beat down their consciences and become kidnappers for it?" (78). The Compromise also compelled supporters and opponents alike to confront the question of states' rights with regard to entering the union as a slave-holding state or not.

8. See also John S. Rock's speech in *The Liberator* (12 March 1858); and Ulrich Bonnell Phillips's *American Negro Slavery.*

9. That Huck repeats gentleman (*commoratio*) and goes on to expand and clarify his definition of quality and aristocracy (*epanados*) aids the audience in its identification with Huck's previous training and experience. His inclusion of the two disparate influences, Widow Douglas and Pap, prove the necessity of his having to articulate what it is he thinks he knows before he can begin to deconstruct it, let alone believe the result of such deconstruction. Of interest, too, is Huck's failure to recognize the significance of Col. Grangerford's name, Saul.

10. For further readings see Abrahams's *Afro-American Folktales,* Zora Neale Hurston's *Mules and Men,* and period fiction.

11. Such identification was not unusual. The most pervasive empathetic identification between African Americans and another culture or race has been with the Jewish people and their plight in Egypt.

12. One truth that has pervaded the psychological conditioning of most African Americans is the blatant discrepancy between White and Other. This discrepancy, especially with the African American Other, remains a significant

factor when believability and trust are the primary issues. It is interesting that during the nineteenth century the suffrage movement under women such as Susan B. Anthony and Elizabeth Cady Stanton as well as women of color such as Sojourner Truth and Anna Julia Cooper made a direct connection between the treatment they received as Other and that received by the southern African American slave.

13. Periodicals, edited by both African Americans and Euro-Americans, recounted slave auctions that resembled the one described here. Twain's own "A True Story" contains the traumatic result of a child's being sold away from his mother. See also his *Autobiography* (5-7).

Chapter 4

1. This prefatory note introduced the "only" voice of the African American, that expressed in spirituals: "Nobody Knows de Trouble I See," "Deep River," "Let My People Go." The study questions that followed this section focused only on religious songs that create mood and deep religious faith, not on physical situation or political and economic conditions.

Bibliography

Abrahams, Roger D. *Afro-American Folktales: Stories from Black Traditions in the New World.* New York: Pantheon Books, 1985.

———. *Deep Down in the Jungle: Negro Narrative Folklore from the Streets of Philadelphia.* Chicago: Aldine, 1970.

———. *Singing the Master: The Emergence of African-American Culture in the Plantation South.* New York: Penguin, 1992.

Appleton, Roy. "Racist Notes Prompt McKinney Inquiry." *Dallas Morning News.* 25 Jan. 1996: 27:31a.

Aptheker, Herbert, ed. *A Documentary History of the Negro People in the United States: From Colonial Times Through the Civil War.* Vol. 1. New York: Citadel, 1951.

Bacon, Francis. *Novum Organum.* Trans. John Gibson. Peru, Ill.: Open Court, 1994.

Bailey, Guy, Natalie Maynor, and Patricia Cukor-Avila, eds. *The Emergence of Black English: Text and Commentary.* Creole Language Library. Vol. 8. Philadelphia: John Benjamins, 1991.

Baker, Houston A., Jr. *Long Black Song: Essays in Black American Literature and Culture.* Charlottesville: UP of Virginia, 1972.

Bakhtin, M. M. *The Dialogic Imagination: Four Essays.* Trans. Caryl Emerson and Michael Holquist. Ed. Michael Holquist. Austin: U of Texas P, 1990.

———. *The Formal Method in Literary Scholarship: A Critical Introduction to Sociological Poetics.* Trans. Albert J. Wehrle. Baltimore: Johns Hopkins UP, 1978.

———. *Problems of Dostoevsky's Poetics.* Trans. Caryl Emerson. Minneapolis: U of Minnesota P, 1984.

Beaver, Harold. "Run, Nigger, Run: *Adventures of Huckleberry Finn* as a Fugitive Slave Narrative." *Journal of American Studies* 8 (1974): 339–61.

Bell, Bernard. "Twain's 'Nigger' Jim: The Tragic Face Behind the Minstrel

Mask." *Satire or Evasion? Black Perspectives on* Huckleberry Finn. Ed. James S. Leonard, Thomas A. Tenney, and Thadious M. Davis. Durham, N.C.: Duke UP, 1992. 124–40.

Bennett, Lerone, Jr. *Before the Mayflower: A History of Black America.* New York: Penguin, 1993.

Berlin, Ira. *Slaves without Masters: The Free Negro in the Antebellum South.* New York: New Press, 1974.

Bingham, Caleb. *The Columbian Orator.* Boston: Baltimore Cushing and Sons, 1837.

Booth, Wayne C. *The Company We Keep: An Ethics of Fiction.* Berkeley: U of California P, 1988.

———. *The Rhetoric of Fiction.* Chicago: U of Chicago P, 1983.

Brooks, Van Wyck. *The Ordeal of Mark Twain.* New York: Dutton, 1920.

Brown, Henry Box. *Narrative of Henry Box Brown who escaped from slavery enclosed in a box 3 feet long, 2 wide and 2 and a half high written from a statement of facts made by himself.* Boston, 1849.

Budd, Louis J. *Mark Twain: Social Philosopher.* Port Washington, N.Y.: Kennikat, 1973.

Burke, Kenneth. *Language as Symbolic Action: Essays on Life, Literature, and Method.* Berkeley: U of California P, 1968.

———. *A Rhetoric of Motives.* Berkeley: U of California P, 1969.

———. *A Grammar of Motives.* Berkeley: U of California P, 1969.

Chadwick-Joshua, Jocelyn. "Say the N-Word and Out You Go: Teaching 'Huck Finn' and Other Racially-Sensitive Literature." *The Critical Response to Mark Twain's Huckleberry Finn.* Ed. Laurie Champion. New York: Greenwood, 1991.

———. "Will We Ever Be Able To Travel Down the Mississippi with Jim and Huck?" *A Teacher's Toolbox: Teaching Strategies for* Adventures of Huckleberry Finn. Connecticut: The Mark Twain Memorial, 1998.

———. *"Blame the Pint! I Reckon I Knows What I Knows": Ebonics, Jim, and New Approaches to Teaching* Adventures of Huckleberry Finn. Durham, N.C.: Duke UP, forthcoming.

Champion, Laurie, ed. *The Critical Response to Mark Twain's Huckleberry Finn.* New York: Greenwood, 1991.

Cooper, Anna Julia. *A Voice from the South by A Black Woman of the South.* 1892. The Schomburg Library of Nineteenth-Century Black Women Writers. New York: Oxford UP, 1988.

Cox, James M. "A Hard Book to Take." *One Hundred Years of* Huckleberry

Finn: *The Boy, His Book, and American Culture.* Ed. Robert Sattelmeyer and J. Donald Crowley. Columbia: U of Missouri P, 1985. 386–403.

de Beauvoir, Simone. *The Second Sex.* Trans. and ed. H. M. Parshley. 1953. New York: Vintage, 1974.

Douglass, Frederick. *Life and Times of Frederick Douglass.* 1892. New York: Macmillan, 1962.

Du Bois, W. E. B. *Black Reconstruction in America, 1860–1880.* 1935. New York: Atheneum, 1992.

Eliot, T. S. "An Introduction to *Huckleberry Finn.*" Rpt. in *Adventures of Huckleberry Finn.* By Mark Twain. Norton Critical Edition. New York: W. W. Norton, 1961.

Ellison, Ralph. "*An American Dilemma*: A Review." *Shadow and Act.* New York: Random House, 1964. 290–302.

———. "Change the Joke and Slip the Yoke." *Partisan Review* 25 (Spring 1958): 212–22. Rpt. in Ellison, *Shadow and Act.* New York: Random House, 1964. 45–59.

———. *Going to the Territory.* New York: Vintage, 1986.

———. *Shadow and Act.* New York: Random House, 1964.

———. "The Uses of History in Fiction: Ralph Ellison, William Styron, Robert Penn Warren, C. Vann Woodward." *Conversations with Ralph Ellison.* Ed. Maryemma Graham and Amritjit Singh. Jackson: UP of Mississippi, 1995. 141–72.

Emerson, Ralph Waldo. Lectures and Biographical Sketches. Ed. J. E. Cabot. New York: Macmillan, 1886. Rpt. 1916.

Fadiman, Clifton. Introduction. *Adventures in American Literature.* Ed. John Gehlmann and Mary Rives Bowman. New York: Harcourt, 1958. 670–72.

Fiedler, Leslie A. "*Huck Finn*: The Book We Love to Hate." *Proteus* 1.2 (Fall 1984): 1–8. Rpt in *Mark Twain's Humor: Critical Essays.* Ed. David E. E. Sloane. New York: Garland, 1993. 217–34.

Fishkin, Shelley Fisher. *Lighting Out for the Territory: Reflections on Mark Twain and American Culture.* New York: Oxford UP, 1996.

———. *Was Huck Black? Mark Twain and African-American Voices.* New York: Oxford UP, 1993.

Foner, Philip S. *Mark Twain: Social Critic.* New York: International P, 1958.

Frye, Northrop. *Anatomy of Criticism: Four Essays.* Princeton: Princeton UP, 1973.

Gates, Henry Louis, Jr., ed. *The Classic Slave Narratives*. New York: Penguin, 1987.

———. "The Blackness of Blackness: A Critique of the Sign and the Signifying Monkey." *Black Literature and Literary Theory*. Ed. Henry Louis Gates, Jr. New York: Routledge, 1990. 285–322.

———. *Figures in Black: Words, Signs, and the "Racial" Self*. New York: Oxford UP, 1989.

———. Foreword. *Iola Leroy, or Shadows Uplifted*. By Frances E. Harper. 1893. The Schomburg Library of Nineteenth-Century Black Women Writers. New York: Oxford UP, 1988.

———. *The Signifying Monkey: A Theory of Afro-American Literary Criticism*. New York: Oxford UP, 1988.

———, ed. *Six Women's Slave Narratives*. The Schomburg Library of Nineteenth-Century Black Women Writers. New York: Oxford UP, 1988.

Gilligan, Carol. *In a Different Voice: Psychological Theory and Women's Development*. Cambridge: Harvard UP, 1982.

Harper, Frances E. *Iola Leroy, or Shadows Uplifted*. 1893. The Schomburg Library of Nineteenth-Century Black Women Writers. New York: Oxford UP, 1988.

Hedrick, Joan D. *Harriet Beecher Stowe: A Life*. New York: Oxford UP, 1994.

Hemingway, Ernest. *Green Hills of Africa*. New York: Charles Scribner and Sons, 1935.

Henry, Peaches. "The Struggle for Tolerance: Race and Censorship in *Huckleberry Finn*." *Satire or Evasion? Black Perspectives on* Huckleberry Finn. Ed. James S. Leonard, Thomas A. Tenney, and Thadious M. Davis. Durham, N.C.: Duke UP, 1992. 25–48.

Hentoff, Nat. *The Day They Came to Arrest the Book*. New York: Laureleaf, 1985.

Hopkins, Pauline. *Contending Forces: A Romance Illustrative of Negro Life in the North and South*. 1900. The Schomburg Library of Nineteenth-Century Black Women Writers. New York: Oxford UP, 1988.

Hughes, Langston, Milton Meltzer, and C. Eric Lincoln. *A Pictorial History of Black Americans*. New York: Crown, 1968.

Hurston, Zora Neale. *Mules and Men: Negro Tales and Voodoo Practices in the South*. 1935. New York: Harper, 1970.

———. *Their Eyes Were Watching God*. New York: Harper & Row, 1937.

Kaplan, Justin. Introduction. *The Adventures of Huckleberry Finn*. By Mark Twain. New York: Random House, 1992.

————. *Mark Twain and His World*. New York: Crescent, 1982.

King, Martin Luther, Jr. *I Have a Dream: Writings and Speeches That Changed the World*. Ed. James M. Washington. San Francisco: Harper, 1992.

Knox, Bernard M. *The Heroic Temper: Studies in Sophoclean Tragedy*. Berkeley: U of California P, 1983.

Lanham, Richard. *A Handlist of Rhetorical Terms: A Guide for Students of English Literature*. Berkeley: U of California P, 1968.

Leonard, James S., Thomas A. Tenney, and Thadious M. Davis, eds. *Satire or Evasion? Black Perspectives on* Huckleberry Finn. Durham, N.C.: Duke UP, 1992.

Major, Clarence. *Juba to Jive: A Dictionary of African-American Slang*. New York: Penguin, 1994.

Mailloux, Steven. *Rhetorical Power*. Ithaca: Cornell UP, 1989.

Marx, Leo. "Mr. Eliot, Mr. Trilling, and Huckleberry Finn," *American Scholar* 22 (Autumn 1953): 423–40. Rpt. in *Huck Finn Among the Critics*. Ed. M. Thomas Inge. Frederick, Md.: University Publications of America, 1985. 113–29.

Meltzer, Milton. *Mark Twain Himself*. New York: Wings, 1960.

"Mississippi Ends Slavery." *Houston Chronicle*. 17 Mar. 1995: A- 15.

Mitchell-Kernan, Claudia. "Signifying." *Mother Wit from the Laughing Barrel*. Ed. Alan Dundes. Jackson: UP of Mississippi, 1990. 310–28.

Morrison, Toni. *Beloved*. New York: New American Library, 1987.

————. *The Dancing Mind*. Speech. Acceptance of the National Book Foundation Medal for Distinguished Contribution to American Letters. 6 Nov. 1996. New York: Knopf, 1997.

————. Interview. "I Come from a People Who Sing All the Time: A Conversation With Toni Morrison." *Humanities* Mar.-Apr. 1996: 7+.

————. Introduction. *Adventures of Huckleberry Finn*. By Mark Twain. Ed. Shelley Fisher Fishkin. New York: Oxford UP, 1996.

————. *Playing in the Dark: Whiteness and the Literary Imagination*. Cambridge: Harvard UP, 1990.

Morson, Gary Saul, and Caryl Emerson, eds. *Rethinking Bakhtin: Extensions and Challenges*. Evanston, Ill.: Northwestern UP, 1989.

Moses, Wilson Jeremiah. *Black Messiahs and Uncle Toms: Social and Literary Manipulations of a Religious Myth*. Pennsylvania: Penn State UP, 1993.

Murray, Albert. *The Hero and the Blues*. Columbia: U of Missouri P, 1973.

Naylor, Gloria. "What Does 'Nigger' Mean?" *Between Worlds: A Reader, Rhetoric, and Handbook*. Ed. Susan Backmann and Melinda Barth. New York: Harper Collins, 1995.

"*New York Gazette* and the Brooklyn Affair." *Mirror of Liberty* 1.1 (Jan. 1839): 2.

Nilon, Charles H. "The Ending of *Huckleberry Finn*: 'Freeing the Free Negro'." *Satire or Evasion? Black Perspectives on* Huckleberry Finn. Ed. James S. Leonard, Thomas A. Tenney, and Thadious M. Davis. Durham, N.C.: Duke UP, 1992. 62–76.

Paine, Albert Bigelow, ed. *Mark Twain's Notebook*. New York: Harper and Brothers, 1935.

Phillips, Ulrich Bonnell. *American Negro Slavery*. New York: Appleton, 1918.

Rasmussen, Kent R. *Mark Twain A to Z: The Essential Reference to His Life and Writings*. New York: Facts on File, 1995.

Roberts, Diane. *The Myth of Aunt Jemima: Representations of Race and Region*. New York: Routledge, 1994.

Robinson, Forrest G. "The Characterization of Jim in *Huckleberry Finn*." *Ninteenth-Century Literature* 43.3 (Dec. 1988): 361– 91.

Schmitz, Neil. "Twain, *Huckleberry Finn* and the Reconstruction." *American Studies* 12 (Spring 1971): 59–67.

Schuyler, George. *Black Empire*. Boston: Northeastern UP, 1991.

———. *Black No More*. Boston: Northeastern UP, 1989.

Schwarz, Benjamin. "What Jefferson Helps to Explain." *Atlantic Monthly*. Mar. 1997: 60–72.

Smiley, Jane. "Say It Ain't So, Huck: Second Thoughts on Mark Twain's 'Masterpiece'." *Harper's* 292.1748 (Jan. 1996): 61–67.

Smith, David L. "Huck, Jim and American Racial Discourse." *Satire or Evasion? Black Perspectives on* Huckleberry Finn. Ed. James S. Leonard, Thomas A. Tenney, and Thadious M. Davis. Durham, N.C.: Duke UP, 1992. 103–20.

Smith, Henry Nash. "A Sound Heart and a Deformed Conscience." *Adventures of Huckleberry Finn*. By Mark Twain. Norton Critical Edition. New York: W. W. Norton, 1977. 363–85.

Snead, James A. "Repetition as a Figure of Black Culture." *Black Literature and Literary Theory*. Ed. Henry Louis Gates, Jr. New York: Routledge, 1990. 59–80.

Stepto, Robert B. "Storytelling in Early Afro-American Fiction: Frederick Douglass's 'The Heroic Slave.'" *Black Literature and Literary Theory*. Ed. Henry Louis Gates, Jr. New York: Routledge, 1990.

Stowe, Harriet Beecher. *The Key to Uncle Tom's Cabin*. Boston: John P. Jewett and Co., 1854.

——. *Uncle Tom's Cabin Or, Life Among the Lowly*. 1852. New York: Penguin, 1986.

Tocqueville, Alexis de. "The Three Races in the United States." *Democracy in America*. Vol. 1. New York: Knopf, 1990.

Trilling, Lionel. Introduction. *Adventures of Huckleberry Finn*. New York: Rinehart, 1948. v-xviii. Rpt. as "The Greatness of *Huckleberry Finn*." *Adventures of Huckleberry Finn*. By Mark Twain. Norton Critical Edition. New York: W. W. Norton and Company, 1962. 310-19.

Twain, Mark. *Adventures of Huckleberry Finn*. 1884. Ed. Michael Patrick Hearn. New York: Clarkson, 1981.

——. *Adventures of Huckleberry Finn*. 1884. Ed. Shelley Fisher Fishkin. New York: Oxford UP, 1996.

——. *The Autobiography of Mark Twain*. Ed. Charles Neider. 1959. New York: Harper Perennial, 1990.

——. *Mark Twain-Howells Letters: The Correspondence of Samuel L. Clemens and William D. Howells, 1872-1910*. Vol. 1. Ed. Henry Nash Smith and William M. Gibson. 2 vols. Cambridge: Harvard UP, 1960.

——. *Mark Twain's Notebooks and Journals*. Ed. Frederick Anderson, Michael B. Frank, and Kenneth M. Sanderson. Vol. 1. Berkeley: U of California P, 1975.

——. *Mark Twain's Notebooks and Journals*. Ed. Robert Pack Browning, Michael B. Frank, and Lin Salamo. Vol. 2. Berkeley: U of California P, 1979.

——. Letter. S. L. Clemens to President James A. Garfield. 12 January 1881. James A. Garfield Papers. Library of Congress.

Valley, John W. "'Huck' and 'Emily' Draw Protesters to Tempe School." *Tempe Informant*. 24 April 1996: 1E.

Walker, Alice. "Writing *The Color Purple*." *In Search of Our Mothers' Gardens: Womanist Prose*. New York: Harcourt, Brace, Jovanovich, 1983.

Wallace, John. *The Adventures of Huckleberry Finn, Adapted*. Virginia: John H. Wallace and Sons, 1985.

——. "The Case Against *Huck Finn*." *Satire or Evasion? Black Perspectives on Huckleberry Finn*. Ed. James S. Leonard, Thomas A. Tenney, and Thadious M. Davis. Durham, N.C.: Duke UP, 1992. 16-24.

————. Editorial. *Chicago Sun Times*. 25 May 1984: A23.

————. "*Huckleberry Finn*: Literature or Racist Trash?" *The Critical Response to Mark Twain's* Huckleberry Finn. Ed. Laurie Champion. New York: Greenwood, 1991. 147–55.

Warren, Kenneth. *Black and White Strangers: Race and American Literary Realism*. Chicago: U of Chicago P, 1993.

Watts, Jerry Gafio. *Heroism and the Black Intellectual: Ralph Ellison, Politics, and Afro-American Intellectual Life*. Chapel Hill: U of North Carolina P, 1994.

Nineteenth-Century African American Periodicals

Douglass' Monthly
The Elevator
The Weekly Advocate/The Colored American
The Mirror of Liberty
The North Star
Freedman's Journal

Index

Varro, 33
Vassa, Gustavas, 16, 64
Voice from the South, A (Cooper), 57
Voltaire, 33

Walker, Alice, 25, 61, 64, 67–68
Wallace, John, 5, 102–03, 133, 134, 137n.1
Wheatley, Phillis, xxii, 64
White League, 103–04

Whittier, John Greenleaf, xxii
Widow Douglas, 34, 64, 84, 85, 112, 119
Wilks sisters, 31, 91, 109–10; slaves of, 35, 110
Wilson, Harriet E., xxii
Wright, Richard, *Native Son*, 25

Young, Robert Alexander, 63